Zakynthos

Brian & Eileen Anderson

Published by
Landmark Publishing
Ashbourne Hall, Cokayne Ave
Derbyshire DE6 1EJ

GW00362225

Zakynthos

Ormos *Ag Georgiou*
Smugglers Cove
Monastery of St George
Gerassimos Cave
Monastery of St Andrew
Porto Vromi
Ormos Vromi
Ormos Stenitis
Anafonitrias Monastery
Volimes
Anafonitria
Ano Volimes
Lighthouse
Korithi
Cape Skinari
Blue Caves
Stenitis
Mycenaean Cemetery
Maries
Skinaria
Orthonies
Askos
Ag Nikolaos
Ferry
Ormos Skiza
Skiza
Exo Hora
Monastery of Spiliotisso
Mikro Nisi
Makris Gialos
Mycenaean Tombs
Kambi
Koroni
Cape Katastari
Ormos Katevasma
Ormos Limniona
Porto Roxa
Louka
Geri
Xayotis Cave
Ormoa Alikon
Agios Leon
Mavri Cave
Katastari
Pigadakia
Alikes
Alikes Beach
Ag Kiriaki Beach
Alikanas
Kalithea
Skoulikado
Alikanas Beach
Ammoudi Beach
Agia Marina
Drakas
Agios Dimitrios
Psarou Beach
Kiliomeno
Agioi Pandes
Kato Gerakari
Drossia Beach
Porto Rouli
Plas Ammos
Agia Marina
Macherado
Callinico Winery (wine tasting)
Amboula Beach
Agalas
Agios Kirikos
Kalipado
Vanato
Planos
Domianou Caves
Mouzaki
Pandokratoras
Sarakinado
Tsilivi
Tsilivi Beach
Cape Keri
Limni Keriou
Lithakia
Sarakini Mansion
Keri
Ambelokipi
Lighthouse
Laganas
Keri Beach
Ormos Keriou
Airport
Boohali
Cape Krioneri
ZAKYNTHOS
Porto Koukla
Laganas Beach
Kalamaki
Argassi Beach
Argassi
Kolpos Lagana
Kalamaki Beach
Ferry to Kilini
Sekania Beach
Kaminia Beach
Porto Zoro
N
W — E
S
Dafni Beach
Ano Vassilikos
Banana Beach
Vassilikos
Plaka Beach
Gerakas Beach
Ag Nikolaos Beach
Porto Roma
Mavratzi Beach

0	1	2	3	4	5 miles
0	1 2 3 4 5 6	7Km			

Zakynthos

Brian & Eileen Anderson

CONTENTS

• LANDMARK HOTSPOTS •

Places not to be missed on Zakynthos

Zakynthos town: Venetian arcaded shopping streets, waterfront atmosphere, castle and interesting squares.

Smugglers Cove: for the amazing sight of a ship embedded in the sand in a beautiful, almost inaccessible beach.

The Blue Caves: a boat trip around these small caves full of luminescent blue water.

Laganas Beach: or the largest beach on the island.

Volimes: for the carpet and lace-makers.

• Feature Boxes •

*I*ntroduction

A late starter in mass tourism, Zakynthos (Zante) has proved that it has all the necessary attributes to succeed. Starting from the back of the pack, it has quickly sliced through the field to become a leading player in a relatively short time. Zakynthos accepted its first charter flight in 1980 and the magic of the island worked instantly. By 1984 mass tourism had taken off in a big way. Now, this sand fringed holiday island combines the charm of unspoilt countryside with all the facilities demanded by the modern tourist.

It was the Venetians who called the island Zakynthos on account of its profuse natural vegetation and fertile soil and they christened it 'Flower of the Levant'. The English adopted the name of Zante but to the Greeks it remains Zakynthos. It is this name which is regularly used on the island and is certain to be encountered, if only on buses heading for Zakynthos town.

Its beaches are perhaps its biggest asset, miles of sand bathed by warm, shallow seas making it ideal for families. With the island's immediate appeal to the tourist, a building boom followed. It quickly realised that being almost last in the field of tourism had an unforeseen advantage. It could steal a march on its competitors by building hotels, restaurants and bars with modern materials to modern standards. The result is a pleasingly up-to-date holiday island with good facilities yet still full of the charm of old Greece. In visual terms, there is probably very little of old Zakynthos to see, the massive earthquake of 1953 (see the feature on p37) made sure of that. Not only did it destroy homes and public buildings but it somehow broke the thread and pattern of life. Old ways, old habits and old customs disappeared with the earthquake only to be reborn in new ways in new surroundings. But the hospitality and charm which characterises Greece is still there and the people of Zakynthos are as friendly, if not more friendly, than elsewhere in the country.

Apart from staking out a spot on the beach to lounge in the sun with a good book to read and a pina colada or a cool beer in hand, there are other things to do on the island should the urge arise. On offer by the tour agencies are a surprising number of tours which include the inevitable round-the-island tour by coach which typically stops at Volimes to see the lace-makers, Anafonitria for the monastery of St Dennis, Macherado for the church of Ag Mavra and Vanato for the Callinico wine factory. The other tour around the island is by boat and there are a surprising number of highlights on this trip which include: the blue caves towards the northern tip of the island where, thanks to light refraction from suspended clay particles in the water, the sea takes on a spectacular, almost luminous, blue colour; Smugglers Cove where a ship smuggling contraband was wrecked in 1976 and now lies half buried in the sand; caves at the southern tip and Marathonisi Island to see the loggerhead turtles.

Most of the other tours on offer leave the island for more distant destinations. Olympia is one such tour and this is easily accomplished in a day, similarly the tour of the neighbouring island of Kefalonia but the trip to Athens usually has an overnight stop in the city.

Most holidaymakers are happy to hire a car for a few days and, if the car tours in this book are followed, four days will get you to all the major points of interest on the island. If a coach trip is preferred, the information for each destination is readily accessed by reference to the index. To help with holiday choices there is also a quick thumbnail sketch of all the major resorts on the island and a good beach guide (p30) to the better beaches on the island. All that remains is to relax, let this book do all the work and concentrate on enjoying Zakynthos to the full.

LOCATION

Zakynthos is the most southern of the six major Ionian islands. The seventh Ionian island, Kythera, lies much further south off the tip of the Peloponnese and is so out of touch with the main group that it is often overlooked as an Ionian

island. Zante's nearest neighbour is Kefalonia, 8.5 nautical miles to the north while the Peloponnese is just 9 nautical miles to the west. In shape, the island roughly resembles an irregular triangle but with a little imagination it can be likened to a scorpion. It covers a land area of 157 sq miles (406 sq km) and the distance from Cape Skinari in the north to Cape Maratha in the south is around 20 miles (32km) as the crow flies but a lot more ground is covered when actually driving between these two points. According to the 1991 census, the island has a population of 35,000 souls.

A chain of hills occupies the western part of the island, from tip to toe, which are high enough to be interesting but rarely dramatic. The highest peak, Mt Vrachionas, lies in the Vrachion massive and reaches an altitude of 2,487ft (758m) above sea level but this is one of only two peaks above 2,300ft (700m). Rivers tend to be seasonal draining away the winter rains shed by the mountains. Most of the cultivable land lies over in the east of the island which is where the majority of the villages are located.

WHEN TO GO

Easter time in April is about the earliest that can be considered. Even at this time there is a risk that the weather will be cold and showery but, if the sun is shining, the island is at its most beautiful. At this time the sea is still cold but the sun is easily hot enough to burn and sunbathers still need to take care. Spring is a delightful season for colour when the trees are vivid green and the wild flowers at their very best. Fortunately, the spring flowers extend into May which is generally more reliable for weather. Daytime temperatures start to rise but the evenings are still cool. It is not always warm enough to dine outside in the evening in the early part of the month but night-time temperatures too are on the rise and it soon becomes possible, well before the month is out. The island has plenty of visitors in these early months but not enough to make it busy with the result that, although bars and tavernas are usually in full swing, some of the water sports have not yet opened.

Things warm up in June in every sense. The days and nights get hotter and the island tourist machine moves into top gear. Nowhere is too crowded and independent visitors can still expect to find accommodation without too much trouble. All that changes in July, with the Greeks and Italians moving into their holiday season, and the island suddenly becomes very crowded. July and August are the hottest months of the year and the least comfortable on the island. The main beaches are full and the facilities often at full stretch.

Even the locals welcome September when the crowds have departed and some of the intense heat leaves the sun. Many regard September as the best month of the summer with the sea still warm and the sun still pouring incessantly from the sky although the autumn rains may well start before the month is out. October is cooler with more cloudy and rainy days but still with fine, sunny periods.

WHERE TO GO

RESORT GUIDE

Holiday brochures try to make each and every resort sound attractive without always revealing too much about its character. This guide offers a quick outline of the main resorts on the island to help in making the most suitable choice. A more detailed description of the resorts may be found by consulting the Out and About section and those marked with an asterisk (*) are also featured in the Good Beach Guide which is included in the next section. Water sport facilities are indicated by symbols. One # indicates very limited facilities, perhaps just pedaloes or simply boats for hire, while the maximum three indicates the whole gamut from paragliding, jet skis, banana rides down to the less energetic pursuits but remember, full facilities are not always available early and late in the season.

All of the significant resorts lie either on the north-east or south coast and none are too far from Zakynthos town. They are presented here by geographical location but the map on p2 shows their exact location.

North-east coast, north of Zakynthos town

Tsilivi*: one of the island's major resorts which is dominated by its huge sandy beach. Plenty of shops and tavernas scattered around the approach roads. A relaxing and good family resort with just about enough high life to keep the night owls happy. ##

Continued on page 12...

Zakynthos Town

Porto Zoro beach

Makris Gialos

Alikanas: a quiet resort based around the village of Alikanas which is above and a little distant from the sea. There is a good beach to hand but resort facilities are still undeveloped. It lies close to the more commercialised Alikes (see below). #

Alikes*: a river divides this resort and some tour operators regard the smaller development south of the river as Alikanas. Predominantly a modern tourist resort but still relatively small. Good facilities and an excellent beach with easy access. Not too much nightlife although there are discos in high season, good for families. ###

South-east coast, south of Zakynthos town

Argassi: this is another of the island's major resort areas and perhaps the least attractive. Its narrow beach is not the best but at least it is away from the main road which runs parallel but a little inland. Little in the way of character and identity. Most of the shops and tavernas straggle along the busy main road, otherwise it's a lively resort which attracts the young set. Good for nightlife.

South coast

Kalamaki: shares the northern end of the Gulf of Lagana. It offers a smaller alternative to Laganas but still with miles of sand, loads of tavernas and nightlife.

Laganas: the island's biggest resort with a wide appeal. A long stretch of sand and facilities of every description; it offers everything from fish and chips and buckets and spades to a sunlounger in a quiet

corner. Good for families but plenty of nightlife around for the young and lively.

GETTING THERE

The easiest way is by charter flight directly from a regional airport in the U K and there are a large number of tour operators offering packages to the island.

For those planning to stay longer than the usual two weeks, it may be necessary to travel on scheduled flights from London to Athens then from Athens to Zakynthos. Usually the journey from the U K can be accomplished in one day without the need for an overnight stop in Athens. There is also a regular bus service from Athens to Zakynthos, around 3 daily, and the journey also includes the ferry crossing from Killini.

The scheduled route into Athens with an onward flight to Zakynthos is the only option from North America, although many Americans find it more economical to fly into London and join a package holiday. Flights from America to Athens may not connect up conveniently with the limited Zakynthos flights. If an overnight stop is required there is a hotel reservations desk at Athens airport.

FOOD AND DRINK

Zakynthos is very modern and cosmopolitan and the fare on offer is much more varied than normally found on a Greek island. It is easily possible to dine on international dishes, from chicken massala to beef vindaloo, without ever touching Greek food but that would rob a holiday of some of its flavour. Even

• MAINLAND AND ISLAND HOPPING •

Zakynthos makes a very convenient base for a two centre holiday but it needs a little planning beforehand. With a hire car, and with permission from the hire company, it is very easy to escape by ferry from Zakynthos town over to Killini in the Peloponnese which instantly opens up a whole new range of possibilities. Here are a few suggestions.

A southern route could incorporate Olympia, easily reached within the first day, and onwards to explore the Mani, the southern central peninsula of the Peloponnese. Mani, a wild and rugged refuge for fugitives in the past, is friendly enough now but the hints of hostility in the castle-like tower houses and the terrain makes this a place apart in Greece. The ruins of medieval Mistra are not that far away and could be incorporated into the return journey.

Using a northern route, Corinth and the Argolid could be a target destination. En route there is a great little rack and pinion railway to try out, from Diakopto on the coast to the mountain village of Kalavrita. The Argolid, stronghold of the Mycenaeans, has an abundance of ancient sites to explore including Mycenae itself and Ancient Corinth. Nafplio or nearby Tolon are ideal bases for exploring this region.

A trip to Delphi is easily accomplished within the day although a one or two night stop is recommended to leave time to absorb and enjoy the site of this ancient oracle. The route from Killini is to head north and ferry over (or very shortly take the bridge) from Rio to Andirio on the northern mainland. From Andirio it is basically a coastal run east to Itea then a short leg inland to Delphi.

the most international of the restaurants usually finds space for some Greek dishes on the menu and there are still a good number of traditional Greek tavernas around.

Just watching the Greeks eat is a pleasure in itself. Seldom do they order individually, instead they order a vast number of communal dishes which fill the table to overflowing. They are far less concerned about cold food and many dishes which arrive hot are cold before they are eaten. Some tourists find it a bit disconcerting when their meals are actually served on the cool side but, in most areas, the message

that tourists generally like their food hot has registered.

Although the tavernas are the traditional eating places, Zakynthos has a selection of restaurants which provide a better standard of decor in particular and offer a more international cuisine. Tavernas and restaurants are obliged to have a menu but many prefer visual alternatives. Diners may be shown a glass show case exhibiting the range of dishes available or, and this is still very common in the villages, they will be led into the kitchen to see exactly what is cooking. If difficulties are experienced in the final choice then

• FAST FOOD ZAKYNTHOS STYLE •

The Greeks are great nibblers, particularly in the mornings, so there is no shortage of fast food.

'Pies' (*pitta*) with various fillings, usually made with filo pastry and looking like a Cornish pasty:-
Tiropitta: cheese. This is the most universally popular and found everywhere.
Spanakopitta: spinach only or with cheese and eggs.
Kreatopitta: minced meat.
Pies for the sweet tooth include:-
Milopitta: apple.
Bougatza: vanilla custard.

Also available are:
Pizza: usually take-away small ones or sometimes sold as pieces.
Souvlaki: small pieces of meat on a wooden skewer served with a lump of bread or with pitta.
Doner me pitta: slices of meat from the *'gyros'* (meat cooked on a vertical spit) placed in a pitta parcel with a little yoghurt, tomato and onion.
Tost: usually a slice of ham and cheese toasted between bread.

Freshly pressed orange juice is widely available.
All the above are traditional Greek take-aways but on Zakynthos there is a much wider range available including baked potatoes with various fillings and chocolate, raisin, almond and pineapple croissants.

spoons may appear for a tasting session. Should there be a menu on the table then it will probably be in Greek and English but it will only show a partial correspondence with the dishes on offer so it still pays to ask. It is unusual to find the table laid, apart from the oil and vinegar flasks, paper napkins and the inevitable toothpicks, but the cutlery arrives with bread after an order is placed.

There is no special form in a taverna and no conventions to follow. The Greeks often go in for a plate of chips and a beer and make it last half the night. For diners though, it is usual to begin with one or a selection of the starters or mezedes on offer. These include tzatsiki (a yoghurt, cucumber and garlic dip), taramasalata (fish roe mixed with potato, oil and vinegar), melitzano salata (an aubergine dip with lemon, garlic and olive oil) and humus, another dip this time from chick peas. Fresh vegetables are rarely available but two vegetables which turn up as mezedes are gigantes (butter beans cooked in tomato and oil) and peas (arakas). Saganaki, fried cheese, is another interesting starter. The waiter will raise an eyebrow if mezedes are ordered separately by each individual, even tourists are expected to order

Ag Nikolaos

Below; Left: Zakynthos Town Right: Olive tree

a selection and share in Greek style. Salads may be preferred as starters or as part of the starters and the most popular is the village salad or *horiatiki salata* which may include lettuce, or cabbage, but often omitted, tomato, onion, cucumber, feta cheese and olives. A few years ago, a salad like this constituted a meal in itself and many tourist were perfectly happy to make a lunch from it. Unfortunately, this made the taverna owner less than happy, consequently the price has risen considerably and they are not always the generous portions they were. Tomatoes, cucumber, feta cheese and lettuce (*maruli*) are all offered as separate dishes. Ready-cooked dishes may include the familiar *moussaka*, a mince dish with aubergines, potato and béchamel sauce; veal in tomato (*kokanisto*), *stifado* (veal stew with onions) or *yiovetsi* (oven cooked lamb served with pasta). Chicken cooked on the spit is popular and inexpensive but favoured amongst the grills is *souvlaki*, veal or pork on a skewer. Chops, pork, lamb or veal, are ever present on the evening menus as are *keftedes* (spicy meat balls) and *biftekia* (mince burgers). Zakynthos specialities include *sofrito*, veal cooked in wine with herbs, garlic and vinegar and served with a thick sauce and *kouneli*, rabbit, which is very popular on the island.

Fish is sometimes on offer but for a selection it is better to find a fish taverna, *psaria taverna*. Fish is becoming increasingly expensive and prices on the menu are often expressed per kilogram which makes them look sky high. In practice, a fish is weighed off and the charge is for that weight. A typical portion is around 14oz (400gm). Lobster

(*astakos*) and red mullet (*barbounia*) are usually top of the menu and are expensive as are shrimps (*garides*). Octopus, grilled or cooked in wine is less expensive as is squid (*kalamari*). At the cheap end is the small whitebait (*marides*) which is eaten in its entirety, head and all. This dish is often available as a starter in a fish restaurant. Desserts are very limited, usually fruit, but the popularity of yoghurt and honey amongst tourists is recognised. If you have tucked into your meal with obvious enjoyment, the proprietor may produce a plate of fruit, peeled and presented with his compliments.

Greek Wines

Some Greeks prefer to drink *ouzo* with meals and this is served in small bottles and usually taken with water. Others choose *retsina,* a resinated wine, which is an acquired taste and the popular commercial brand is Kourtaki. Most wine lists contain some of the country's acknowledged good wines like Boutari Naoussa and Lac des Roches as well as some medium priced popular ones like Kambas, Rotonda and Domestica. Zakynthos grows plenty of vines and has wine manufacturers but the locals still make their own which is usually good and much cheaper than the branded labels. Ask for '*krasi dopio*' (local wine) or '*spitiko krasi*' (house wine) which is usually served in a carafe or metal jug.

PEOPLE AND CULTURE

In spite of the island's turbulent history and a parade of different masters over the centuries, the people of Zakynthos have retained their own brand of Greekness. This Greekness, tempered by western influences, from the Venetians, the French and the British, over the centuries, is a little different from that observed in the more easterly parts but the language and the church provided a continuity which has kept the people in touch with their own identity. Their conviviality and hospitality to strangers wins the island many friends. Sadly, these qualities are subdued by the pressure of work in the height of the tourist season but never squashed. Away from all the bustle, it takes only a cheerful greeting, sometimes only a smile, to be on the receiving end of their hospitality. It may take the form of an orange pulled from a bag or a handful of freshly grown broad beans but whatever it is, it is considered bad manners to refuse. Language barriers don't exist for the Greeks and mostly they will chatter away in their native tongue in the full expectancy that you will understand some or part of whatever they are saying. Body language and gesticulations play a full part too.

The family unit is strong and still the basis of Greek society, although there are signs that the bonds are starting to weaken under western influences. It is sons who receive the adulation and are totally spoilt by their parents. This does not mean that daughters are not welcomed, as in some societies, and the ideal family is regarded as one son and one daughter. Parental influence is still strong when the time is right for their children to marry. Arranged marriages have not entirely disappeared. They are no longer the norm but parents still have a dominant role in satisfying the demands of society and tradition. It is the duty of the son to stand by his parents to ensure that suitable matches are made for all his sisters before he can contemplate marriage. Although a dowry is no longer a legal requirement, and this repeal was only in recent times, it is still perpetuated. A girl goes into marriage often with the gift of a furnished house or apartment from her parents. It remains the girl's property and her security. In the same way gifts of gold to the bride, also to provide for her security, are not unusual. At least the newly wedded couple start life without the burden of debt and are able to build and plan a future for their own children. The family unit extends into business too. The Greek preference is for self employment or failing that a secure job with the state. Most small businesses employ only family and are eventually passed down via sons and daughters.

It is still a male dominated society but attitudes are slowly changing amongst the younger generation. Just a short time ago, only young men had the freedom to go out alone but this too has changed and young women are now part of the social scene. The role of women in the broader society has been recognised in legislation. They acquired the vote only in 1952 and the first woman Deputy was elected to Parliament the following year. Sexual discrimination in career opportunities and in the place of work has been outlawed. Many

Geri

Volimes

practical steps have been taken to assist the integration of women as equals in society. Low cost nurseries providing child places have been provided to free women to work and they have acquired rights of ownership after marriage and an equal share of communal property on divorce. Women now hold important posts in all branches of the Civil Service and in commerce but, in spite of all their progress, equality is only accepted in the big cities. Throughout rural Greece it remains contrary to the culture and fundamental change will only be fully accepted very slowly. For women travelling alone in Greece there are no exceptional problems. The incidence of violent crime, including rape, is much lower than in other western societies. But it is not unknown and the same wariness of the possible situations should be observed, especially in a large city. Greek men firmly believe they are irresistible to all women so their attentions can be expected.

ARTS

Music and dance have always played a role in Zakynthian life which is perhaps why the islanders embraced so heartily the new cultural expressions which arrived with the Venetians. The first school of music was opened on the island in 1815 by an Italian, Professor Marco Battaglia, and shortly afterwards the first brass band was formed. Even today this remains a strong tradition and the island has a philharmonic orchestra and a choir as well as a number of bands which parade on festival days. Zakynthos over the years has produced many fine musicians who

have become well known throughout the country.

Greek Dancing

Dancing, the men claim, is in their blood and they need little encouragement to demonstrate some of the fine local folk dances. The most famous of these is the Zakythian *syrtos*, a lively dance in two-four time, which is often known by different names in the various villages. Dance, like music, is often the highlight entertainment at a religious festival. In tourist resorts local dancers often perform in restaurants and tavernas throughout the season. Many dances local to Zakynthos are performed but programmes usually include the more popular dances from around the country.

FLORA AND FAUNA

Flowers abound in spring from the ubiquitous Spanish broom to rare wild orchids but the best time to see them is from late March through April into May although the season persists longer around the mountain tops.

Much of the island is very fertile and the cultivation of olives, citrus fruit, vines, figs and vegetables are important to the economy. The Venetians called the island 'Flower of the Levant' perhaps more with its fertility in mind than, as is often supposed, its profusion of wild flowers. Spring, late March to early May, is the best time to see the colourful parade of flowers which include muscari, ornithogalums, geraniums and a number of wild orchids. By the end of May, the heat and the dryer conditions rapidly bring a close to the main display but there are always some that remain in flower to delight visitors, like the electric blue flowers of wild chicory, *Chicorium intybus*, often seen sprawling by the wayside or the delicate white flowers sprouting an abundance of pink stamens of the wild caper, *capparis spinosa*. These delicate flowers seem incongruous on such a tough, spiny shrub.

Despite the heat and the lack of water in summer, a few flowers usually manage to keep going, especially on the shrubs. The pink-flowered cistus, *Cistus creticus*, reserves its best display for spring but manages to produce a succession of its short-lived, crinkle petalled flowers throughout much of the summer. Mulleins too seem indestructible and their tall yellow spikes seem to survive in the heat and drought. Only seen in summer is the beautiful sea daffodil, *Pancratium maritimum*, which has made the sand dunes its own special habitat.

Autumn rains bring out the crocus and cyclamen in a new flush of flowers which help to keep winter colourful until spring gets into its stride once again.

The fauna is surprisingly good too and the island has a wide range of wild animals including foxes, hares, weasels, pine martens, rabbits, hedgehogs and tortoise. The latter two are most likely to be seen on the road, hedgehogs mainly dead but not usually tortoise. Greek

• THE MONK SEAL •

The sea around Zakynthos, especially along the rocky west coast, is frequented by the rare and endangered monk seal, *Monachus monachus* which thrives in the warm waters of the Mediterranean and Atlantic off the coast of North Africa.

Mentioned by Homer, they were much more prolific in the ancient world but have been disturbed over recent centuries by the loss of breeding habitats and by conflict with fishermen. This rather shy animal takes refuge in caves and remote places out of sight of man to give birth to young, usually a single pup. Tourist development along the coast and increased leisure activity around the sea shores have seriously interfered with the regular haunts of this species.

The monk seal lives on fish and octopus but, with ever diminishing supplies, it has brought them into direct competition with fishermen. Too many times in the past has the conflict been resolved simply by killing the seal, especially when they get caught up in nets. Now the emphasis is strictly on conservation and the World Wildlife Fund supports a project to conserve a small population of these seals which is known to exist in an area around northern Zakynthos, Kefalonia, Ithaka and Lefkas.

drivers believe it unlucky to kill tortoise and go to great trouble to avoid them. It is surprising that the rabbit population is still good since they figure prominently on the menu on Zakynthos.

Snakes are around too in numbers but mostly harmless. Vipers are known to exist but are unlikely to be encountered.

The species which Zakynthos is perhaps most famous for is the loggerhead turtle, *Caretta caretta*, which nests on its beaches (see feature on p53). Monk seals, another rare species, also inhabit the water in the quieter northern parts of the island.

HISTORY

The island's role in very early history does not appear to have been significant. It is very likely that Zakynthos was inhabited in Neolithic times but, unlike its northern neighbour, Kefalonia, there is not so much evidence around to appreciate the importance of these populations.

According to the Greek historian Herodotus, writing in the fifth century BC, the first settlers to reach Zakynthos were led by Zakynthos, son of King Dardanos. They arrived around 1600-1500BC from the Arcadian city of Psophis in the Peloponnese and called the island Zakynthos. With memories of home still strong, the new stronghold built on the hill where the castle behind Zakynthos town now stands was called Psophis.

The island's role in Mycenaean times is unclear but Mycenaean rock tombs and a cemetery have been located on the western coast. There are no remains of strongly built cities similar to those seen on Kefalonia and even references to the island in Homer's Odyssey are slight: twenty of Penelope's suitors were said to come from Zakynthos. Nor does the island appear to have been involved in the Trojan war in the thirteenth century BC.

THE PELOPONNESIAN WAR

Zakynthos does not really enter the history books until a much later period, until the outbreak of the Peloponnesian War (431-404BC) which started as a dispute between Corfu (*Kerkyra*) and Corinth and ended up involving Athens and Sparta. Zakynthos joined Corfu on the side of Athens and sent ships to reinforce the Corfiot navy. In 430BC they were involved directly in the action when the Spartan admiral Knemos laid siege to the city of Zakynthos. In spite of strong support by a sizeable fleet, he was unable to overcome the fierce resistance and forced to retire. In 418BC, Zakynthians were involved in the ill-fated attempt by Athens to subjugate Sicily which resulted in a tremendous loss of ships and men. Athens managed to rebuild its navy but was seriously weakened by the affair which eventually led to the end of the Peloponnesian War when it finally capitulated to Sparta in 404BC.

The Spartans promptly moved in to take charge of Zakynthos and the democratic system of rule which had developed on the island was pushed aside by the victors. Democracy was restored fairly soon afterwards, in 371BC, by a treaty signed in Athens which granted the right of autonomy to Greek cities. Throughout the fourth century BC there was a greater inclination for co-operation between city states creating new power bases in Greece. In this period, the Aetolian league was formed which Zakynthos, like its neighbour Kefalonia, joined. Eventually, with its new-found strength, it engaged in acts of piracy taking riches from the Achaeans (Peloponnese) until the Achaeans formed their own league around 225BC.

In the meantime, a new and powerful force was growing which was set to shape the whole destiny of the country. Until the second half of the fourth century, Macedonia's role in Greek politics had been very limited but all that was to change, especially when Philip II came to the throne in 357BC. He built up a strong and well-trained army and was easily able to defeat his hostile neighbours. Turning his attention to the south, he marched down on Athens in 338 BC. Zakynthos managed to keep out of this particular war but, eventually, the Achaean League turned to the now powerful Macedonia for help. King Philip V, recognising the strategic importance of these islands, attacked and captured Zakynthos in 217BC.

THE ROMAN PERIOD

Around this time, Rome and Carthage were engaged in the Second Punic War which lasted from 218-202BC and Philip V of Macedonia allied himself with the Carthaginian general Hannibal.

Ag Nikolaos

Venetian arcade, Zakynthos Town

Rome emerged victorious and promptly turned attention to the problem of Philip. With help from the eastern Mediterranean cities, they quickly overpowered Philip and the Roman colonisation of Greece had begun.

Kefalonia was taken by the Romans around 189BC but it was not fully able to take Zakynthos which became a battle ground for a period. An insurrection by the people, backed by the Aetolians, brought a fierce reaction by the Romans who promptly sacked the island. Finally, around 150BC, the Romans took full possession of Zakynthos. Slowly the island accepted the Romans and actually fought alongside them to successfully defend Zakynthos around 70BC when it was threatened by King Mithridates of Pontus (a kingdom on the Black Sea) who was engaged in war with Rome.

Piracy was so strong in this period that the pirates had virtual control of the seas and it was difficult even for the Roman armies to sail to Greece. Zakynthos, like the other Ionian islands, suffered repeated raids by Sicilian corsairs. Stirred into action by 67BC, Rome charged Pompey (who later became Pompey the Great) with the task of ridding the seas of these pirates which he successfully accomplished. In the reorganisation which followed, Zakynthos became part of the province of Achaia which included virtually all of present mainland Greece.

THE BYZANTINE PERIOD (AD337-1267)

By AD337, the Roman empire had grown so large that it started to divide into the Latin-speaking west and the Greek-speaking east, especially following the formation of the new Christian capital of Byzantium by the Emperor Constantine (later known as Constantinople). Zakynthos was included in the eastern section which later became Byzantium. The two parts of the empire had just one emperor until 396.

From the late fourth - seventh centuries, Barbarian tribes from Europe, namely the Vandals and Goths were mounting piratical raids against the Roman Empire. Zakynthos, like other Ionian islands, suffered at their hands as well as from the Arabic Saracens. A particularly serious attack by the Visigoths and Huns in 395 laid waste to Zakynthos and it required an intervention of the Emperor Theodosius' troops to recover the island.

Maries

It is believed that Christianity came early to Zakynthos and there is a legend that Mary Magdalene visited the island while travelling from Jerusalem and Rome and spent some time preaching the teachings of Jesus. The village of Maries, near where Mary landed, still celebrates every year with a festival to mark the event.

Raids continued unabated and when it was not the Barbarian tribes causing the damage, it was sickness. In 591 the island fell victim to the plague which was sweeping through the Empire. To counter trouble from these repeated attacks, Emperor Heraclius reorganised the administrative themes in 629-634 into smaller units more able to organise themselves. Zakynthos was assigned to the Theme of Lombardy of which Kefalonia was the head. By combining fleets, the Theme of Lombardy was reasonably successful in fighting off Arab attacks and a period of relative prosperity developed which lasted until the theme was dismantled early in the ninth century. This unpopular move was corrected in 887 when a new theme recognised the Ionian islands as a natural group headed again by Kefalonia. This theme lasted for 300 years.

By the eleventh century, events and changes in Europe were posing new threats from the Normans who were pushing into this part of the world. In 1081 the Normans, under Robert Guiscard, took Corfu and his son continued south to capture Kefalonia and Zakynthos but failed to overcome the resistance of the islanders. Within three years the Byzantines, backed by a now powerful Venice, were able to recover Corfu and dispel the Norman threat from the region. In return Venice was granted certain trading privileges in the region. There was no lasting peace, for the island was again attacked by the Normans and the Genoese. After taking Zakynthos and all the Ionians in 1147, the Normans were driven out by the Byzantine Emperor Manuel with the

help of the Venetians but the islands were handed back to the Normans as part of a deal for a peace in 1185. The former corsair, Admiral Margaritus, took control of Kefalonia, Ithaka and Zakynthos and set up his headquarters in St George's castle on Kefalonia.

THE ORSINI FAMILY (1194-1357)

Admiral Margaritus was succeeded by Matthios Orsini in 1194 who abolished the Greek Orthodox church in favour of Catholicism to gain favour with the pope and dismissed the Greek Orthodox bishop. The Byzantine Empire finally crumbled as a result of the Fourth Crusade (1202-4). Thanks to help offered to the Crusades, the Venetians gained control of a number of territories along its trade route to the Levant which included the Ionian islands although they did not gain immediate control.

Orsini, once a pirate himself, was nothing if not cunning. By 1209 he decided it was in his best interests to change sides so declared servitude to the Venetians and pacified the Vatican with the promise of a yearly tribute.

In 1258 he was succeeded by his son, Ricardo, who was no less devious than his father. With the growing power of Theodore Angelos Comnenos, Despot of Epirus, Ricardo took steps to guard his own interests by marrying his son, Ioannes, to Comnenos' daughter. Ioannes Orsini, cast in the same mould, took control on his father's death. Murder and intrigue within the family followed but the Orsinis held on to power up until 1357. In the final years, Ioannes II, who had murdered his brother, renounced the Orsini lineage and adopted the name Ioannes Angelos Comnenos to court popularity. His most serious mistake was to usurp his sister's dowry, the property of her husband, William Tocco, which was half the island of Zakynthos.

THE TOCCO DYNASTY (1357-1479)

In 1335 Ioannes Angelos Comnenos was poisoned by his wife. In 1357, the King of Naples gave the islands of Kefalonia, Ithaka, Zakynthos and Lefkada to Leonard I Tocco. After years of Orsini rule and high taxation, Zakynthos was in a poor state but Leonard adopted a softer policy to advance the welfare and prosperity of the island. This policy survived only as long as Leonard for his successor, Carlo I, already holding land in Epirus, proved to be a greedy and violent ruler until his death in 1429. By this time Venice was engaged in constant running battles with the Turks who were advancing into mainland Greece. Under pressure from the Turks, Carlo II ceded the town of Ioannina to them but they were not appeased and, in 1442, the Turks laid siege to and sacked Zakynthos.

In 1448, Leonard III came to power, the last in a line of five successive Tocco rulers. It was he who returned the rights of the Greek Orthodox church in 1454 and invited the clergy to elect a Greek Orthodox bishop of Kefalonia and Zakynthos whose episcopal see was based in Kefalonia. His fortunes in the constant battles with the Turks ebbed and flowed but he was forced to yield Kefalonia to the Turks in 1484 but the Venetians were allowed to keep Zakynthos on condition of a yearly tax of 500 ducats to the sultan.

VENETIAN RULE (1484-1797)

Turkish control of the area proved to be short lived. Backed by Spain, Venice launched an attack on Kefalonia in 1500 to dispel the Turks. They laid siege to the castle of St George, captured it and slaughtered the Turkish garrison. The Venetians were welcomed as liberators by the inhabitants but they merely exchanged one master for another. Now Venice was firmly in control in the Ionian islands. Rule was invested in noblemen who sought to strengthen the island by encouraging immigrants, a policy fully supported by Venice. Indeed, Venetians wishing to settle in Zakynthos were promised privileges and tax exemption. Zakynthos was something of a special case since it had been virtually deserted after the battles with the Turks, many of the inhabitants having fled. Now the population multiplied, farms were organised and a merchant fleet developed for trade. Records show that the population grew quickly to reach some 20,000 in 1515. A hierarchical system of administration was used throughout the Ionian islands, the highest ranking Venetian nobleman on the island was appointed Prevedore. He had overall control but responded to the Prevedore of the Ionian islands whose seat was on Corfu. Apart from the nobility, other classes were recognised, namely the *civilii*, the citizens, who were represented by the middle class merchants, priests, teachers, professional men and the like and the *populari*, the common people. Labourers and

Swallowtail butterfly,
Paplio machaon

Oleander

Wild roses

farmers made up the latter class. There were many beneficial aspects of the Venetian rule, they introduced farm reforms and encouraged the production of olives for oil, introduced art and music and generally raised the level of civilisation. On the whole, the inhabitants of the Ionian islands fared better under the Venetians than the Greeks under Turkish rule.

Troubled times still existed, especially in 1537 when Suleiman the Magnificent declared war on Venice. Zakynthos, like Kefalonia, suffered at the hands of Barbarossa, one-time pirate then admiral of the Turkish fleet, and again in 1571 when the Algerian admiral Uluzeli unsuccessfully laid siege to the island.

Zakynthos and the other Ionian islands supported Venice in the Cretan war (1645-69) in which the Turks emerged as victors and Venice was forced to sign a peace treaty in which they relinquished Crete but, as part of the bargaining, were released from paying the annual tribute for Zakynthos. Many Cretan refugees settled on Zakynthos bringing with them their own traditions which served to enrich the island's own customs. Included amongst those refugees were the forebears of the Greek poet Dionysios Solomos.

The seventeenth century saw the start of a series of earthquakes far worse than the island had previously known and Zakynthos was also struck again by the plague in 1688 which decimated the population.

Venice, a great power throughout this period was, by the start of the eighteenth century, heading into decline. Exhausted by its long struggles, Venice was finally defeated by Napoleon in 1797 and Zakynthos, like the other Ionian islands, became a French possession.

FRENCH AND RUSSIAN MASTERS (1797-1809)

The French were greeted with excitement and they responded by outlawing the now hated aristocratic system of rule. In the following year, disaster overtook the French fleet at the Battle of Abukir after which they were forced to yield the Ionian islands to the Russians and the Turks. The first action of the Russo-Turkish regime was to restore the aristocratic system of administration. In a joint declaration by the Russian and Turkish admirals, the Ionian islands were joined to become one nation, the Septinsular Republic. Fourteen delegates made up the governing senate and eventually a constitution was drawn up which acknowledged the fact that the Republic was a Russian protectorate.

By the treaty of Tilsit, in 1807, the Ionian islands were ceded back to France who were again greeted warmly. Once again the French occupation was doomed to be short-lived but this time the threat came from Britain.

THE BRITISH RULE (1809-1864)

In 1809, Britain mounted a blockade of the Ionian islands as part of the war against Napoleon and, on 19 September of the same year, hoisted the British flag over Zakynthos castle. Kefalonia and Ithaka quickly surrendered and the British installed provisional governments. Work to improve the infrastructure of the island, including roads and sanitation, received priority and the British were popular in the short term. The position of the British was formalised by the Treaty of Paris in 1815 which recognised the United States of the Ionian islands and decreed that it become a British protectorate.

Thomas Maitland, the first Lord High Commissioner in 1815 with a seat in Corfu, devised a constitution for the Ionians which concentrated power in his own hands. Although he continued with many public works to improve the infrastructure and protect and encourage trade, he was disliked for his autocratic ways. Resistance groups started to form and they petitioned King George IV of England asking for a revision of the oppressive constitution but to no avail. Succeeding Lord High Commissioners were often better received than Maitland but, nevertheless, the opposition to British rule was slowly organised and a Zakynthos Fighting Committee formed. Much of their energy in the early years was directed to supporting the Greeks in their revolution against the Turks.

By 1848 the resistance movement was gaining strength and turning against the British, not just on Zakynthos but throughout the Ionian islands. Skirmishes between the people and the British army in Argostoli and Lixouri on Kefalonia led to some relaxation of the laws including a greater freedom for the press and the granting of additional civil rights. Under the new freedoms political parties were allowed and three formed on Zakynthos, the Radicals, the Reformers and the Plutocrats. The Radicals wanted to be rid of the English whilst the

Reformers advocated improved government under the English and the Plutocrats were so pro-British they were regarded as nothing more than tools of the English. Underlining this division of opinion was the fact that the island had reached a level of prosperity never previously experienced. Many good public works had been carried out and many of the bridges built at the time still continue to serve the island's road system.

Free elections were held on 28 February 1850 for the Ionian parliament. The business concerning the house soon after its formation was union with Greece. This brought further reprisals from the British but union with Greece was now a declared aim and a growing restlessness resulted in still more skirmishes. Zakynthos, along with the other Ionian islands, were ceded to Greece as a gesture of goodwill when the British-backed Prince William of Denmark became King George I of the Hellenes.

UNION WITH GREECE (1864)

Although sharing the same history as Greece after union, economic and social conditions treated the island unfavourably. Zakynthos declined for much of the early part of the twentieth century and its grandeur faded. Particularly damaging was the massive earthquake of 1953 (see feature P37) which completely obliterated all traces of its illustrious past. In the present day, prosperity is steadily returning to the island in the form of tourism.

A day out on a different beach provides a refreshing change and the purpose of this guide is to help with choices. It is not intended to be a comprehensive list but includes only those beaches with good features which reward the effort of getting there. Sandy beaches are selected in the main but outstandingly good shingle beaches are also included. Refer to the map on p2 for locations and for ease of reference they are listed in clockwise order starting from Zakynthos town. Further details may be found by consulting the car tours on p46.

Porto Zoro

Porto Zoro: picturesque enclosed bay where projecting rocks at one end add further character. The deep beach itself is of excellent sand with just some fine shingle on the shore line. Slopes only gently into the sea, good for paddling. There is a taverna down at sea level with beach beds and shades for hire. Sea sports include pedaloes, jet skis and speedboats.

Banana

Banana: it is not the most inspiring name for a very beautiful and long stretch of fine sand but so called because it is shaped like a banana. Tavernas are set above the beach at either end and there are sun beds and shades available for hire. Thatched parasols add a touch of the Caribbean. Jet skis and other water sports in season, very popular in the height of summer and crowded. It is not the easiest beach to find but directions are included in car tour 1.

Ag Nikolaos

Ag Nikolaos: an extensive area of fine grey sand lapped by a shallow sea. Very popular beach for water sports and there is a free coach service laid on from Argassi and Laganas. Tends to be a bit noisy with the young, sporty set in action but there is a quieter end with a small, sheltered bay. Plenty of facilities with bars, cafés and snacks available as well as sun beds and umbrellas. This is the place for an exhilarating ringo or banana ride.

Gerakas

Gerakas: a long, long sandy beach with plenty of depth in a shallow bay. This is one of the main loggerhead turtle beaches (see feature p53); as a consequence there are no water sports, except for pedaloes, and no facilities down at beach level but there are tavernas, and bars on the approach road. Sun shades and beds are available on this good family beach but note that the beach

is out of bounds in the evenings to protect the turtles, especially throughout the breeding season.

Kalamaki

Kalamaki: this is the quieter end of Lagana Bay. Fine dark sand with a clear shallow sea and bounded by low cliffs to the northern end. Beach furniture is available in the form of sun beds and umbrellas whilst adjacent to the beach is a hotel which offers bar facilities. Most of the eating places are on the road which leads down to the beach. Not too much in the way of water sports since speed boats are banned in the bay to protect the loggerhead turtles but pedaloes are available. Good for families.

Laganas

Laganas: the longest and perhaps the busiest beach on the island. The dark grey-brown sand often gets quite compacted which makes for easy walking. It is away from the main road so there is no problem with traffic noise and it is never necessary to wander far in search of refreshments since bars and tavernas of all description face directly onto the beach. Sun beds and umbrellas are freely available but water sports are limited by the ban on speedboats operating in the bay on account of the danger to the loggerhead turtles. It still manages a lively atmosphere with pedaloes riding the sea and boat trips on offer. Those seeking a little more peace can wander to the southern end.

Alikes

Alikes: an attractive sweep of bay divided by two small jetties. Pale golden and fine, the sand is of good quality and, although the beach is not too deep it stretches far enough not to get too crowded. Plenty of facilities for eating and drinking on hand and the usual beach furniture of beds and umbrellas are available for hire. Much favoured by families for its gently shelving beach and good too for water sports with the whole gamut from paragliding, jet skis, water skis to ringo and banana rides, pedaloes and canoes. There are even beach bikes for hire.

Alikanas

Alikanas: a more natural beach for those looking for peace and quiet. An intimate, narrow stretch of fine sand, limited access and parking. Very little in the way of facilities but there are beach beds and parasols.

Amboula

Amboula: a good stretch of fine golden sand in a quiet setting, shaded in parts with tamarisk trees; some shingle by sea edge. There is a beach bar and beach shower to hand as well as sun beds and umbrellas for hire.

Tsilivi

Tsilivi: Picturesque bay with a long, long stretch of fine sand which shelves only gently into the sea which makes it good for families. A small fishing harbour occupies the northern end. There is a scattering of bars and tavernas facing directly onto the beach and there are sun beds and umbrellas available for hire. Plenty of water sports and easy access to the beach are further plus points.

• LANDMARK TIPS •

1. Beach Beds

The cost of hiring sun beds and umbrellas is overpriced and seems to climb each year. The total cost over a full two week holiday can be quite significant. A full day's rate is charged even if the loungers are used for only a couple of hours. One alternative is to buy beach umbrellas and air beds which are freely available in the shops. Their cost will be recovered in just two or three days and, if luggage space is tight when departing, it is no loss if they are passed on to some newly arrived holidaymakers.

2. Bars with Pools

Watch out for purpose built bars with swimming pools which offer all the facilities free to customers, including free use of sun beds and parasols, providing drinks and food are bought from the bar. Prices are not usually elevated and many of these sell good value bar snacks. It is a growing market and a number of hotels are following the trend and also offer their swimming pool and facilities free on the same basis.

3. Frappe

Hot drinks lose their appeal when the weather is very hot and a more suitable drink for coffee fans is iced coffee or *frappe*. It is very easy to make and self-catering visitors can put one together in a trice. Plastic *frappe* makers, nothing more than a plastic container with lid, can be bought cheaply but an empty coffee jar with lid is ideal. For one cup add a normal measure of instant coffee, ice cubes, milk and sugar if taken, and a cup of chilled water. Shake vigorously to dissolve the coffee, around 30 seconds, pour into a glass and it should have a good head of froth. For some reason, it tastes better drunk through a straw.

4. Museums and Archaeological Sites

Except for private museums, there is often no charge on Sundays for entry to many museums and archaeological sites throughout Greece.

Out and About

*P*ART 2: A day out in Zakynthos town

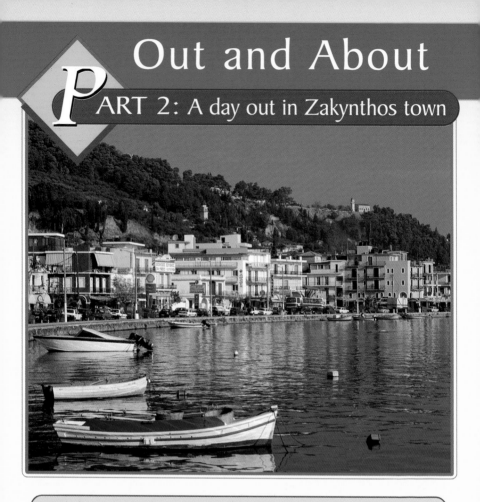

Zakynthos town spreads thinly along the waterfront, the steep slopes of the hill behind restricting any real depth of development. The location of the hill has dictated the town's spread of growth, its nucleus being more towards the northern end of the harbour directly below the castle. Most of the main points of interest can be found here, within a short distance of Solomos Square. A visit will take a pleasant half a day with maybe a little more time if a visit to the castle is intended.

Very little is known about the history of Zakynthos before the Hellenistic period, although ancient writings suggest the island was inhabited in prehistoric times. There has been a fortification of some kind

34

The main points of interest are:

- The Church of St Nicholas on the Mole
- Library
- Byzantine Museum
- Solomos Square
- St Mark's Square

- The Church of St Dionysios (Dennis)
- Shopping in the area of Alexandrou Roma
- Harbour front - Strata Marina
- The Castle

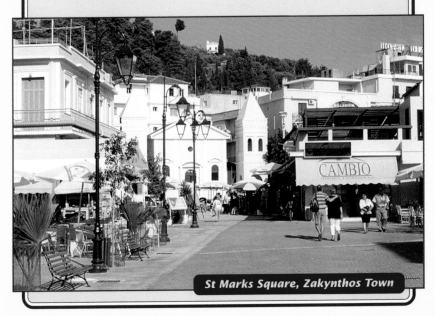

St Marks Square, Zakynthos Town

on the site of the present castle for 3,500 years. Its geographical position on the eastern coast provides sheltered anchorage and a defensible hilltop site with easy access to cultivable land. A site not easily matched elsewhere on the island; the rocky western coast being more exposed to the elements and Laganas Bay too shallow for shipping.

Unlike neighbouring Kefalonia, where there is tangible evidence of Mycenaean occupation, most of Zakynthos' early history is lost in the mists of time. A cluster of Mycenaean tombs on the west coast lend credence to accounts of a Mycenaean presence on the island though and there are Homeric references to Zakynthos in the Odyssey. It is thought the Venetians stripped the island of any antiquities there were and took them back to Venice, like a marble group depicting Apollo, Aphrodite and Artemis found near the present castle. This could partly account for a lack of many 'finds' but the island was also constantly plundered up to that time.

When the Venetians arrived, the town was enclosed within the walls of a medieval castle on the acropolis site. This was later replaced by the Venetian fortress whose walls still girdle the hilltop. The Venetian fortress no longer dominates the skyline above the town. Its walls are now masked by pine wood, planted after the ruins inside had been cleared.

Once the threat of pirate raids was brought under control in the sixteenth century, the townspeople moved away from the protection of the fortress walls down to the narrow stretch of land along the shore below which became known as Hora (town). As part of harbour improvements, instigated by the British in 1815, work was started on building a new quay on the north side. This was to take 75 years to complete, by which time the British had long since gone and Zakynthos was part of Greece. Before 1815 the church of St Nicholas on the Mole, in Solomos Square, was on an islet, connected to the land by a bridge. The resulting land infill joined up the island with the land and created what is now Solomos Square.

During this time, Zakynthos was developing into a town of some style with graceful arcaded streets, notable public buildings and distinctive mansions. The British occu-pation, in the first half of the nineteenth century, brought about many improvements to the infrastructure. Of prime importance was attention to the water supply and sanitation, which improved the living standards of the poorer section of the community especially. A network of roads was constructed, bridges built and street lighting installed all of which encouraged commercial expansion. The Zakynthians, in keeping with their Ionian neighbours, also aspired to a higher level of cultural activity than in other parts of Greece. Zakynthos boasted a rather grand municipal theatre where touring opera companies from Italy regularly performed. There was also a growing number of dramatic performances in Greek. Interest and enjoyment in such forms of entertainment was not the exclusive domain of the upper classes. It was an interest shared by a large proportion of the population as a whole. One story relates how a local peasant, who had been sat on the steps outside listening to a performance of a Verdi opera in Italian, stopped the Prima Donna as she was leaving. After complimenting her on her singing, he pointed out the exact point where she had muffed her notes.

Zakynthos enjoyed its heyday as a seat of gracious living during the nineteenth century. After union with Greece and the departure of colonial influences, things were never the same again. There was a gradual decline in prosperity which was hastened by a couple of World Wars and a civil war in the twentieth century.

Continued on page 40...

• THE EARTHQUAKE OF 1953 •

The Zakynthians were not completely unprepared for the earthquake of 12th August 1953, only for the extent of the devastation. A couple of strong tremors during the preceding days had alerted the population to the danger. So much so, that many abandoned their homes to live in the open. The strongest tremor, which registered 7.5 on the Richter scale, swept up through Zakynthos and Kefalonia. An eyewitness account tells of the rippling effect of the tremor's approach. Of how he looked round to see people dancing like puppets and then suddenly found himself being tossed helplessly about.

Zakynthos town and island were reduced to rubble. Unfortunately for Zakynthos town, what the earthquake did not destroy the ensuing fire consumed. The gracious Venetian squares and campaniles of the town were obliterated along with most of its historical records and artefacts. Without the enterprise of one man, Nikos Varvanis, who with a few helpers rescued what he could of the island's heritage from the devouring flames, there would have been even less to show of its past. Fortunately, loss of life was limited because of the warning tremors beforehand. The British were first on the scene to help the inhabitants by organising shelters and restoring some of the infrastructure.

After such complete devastation the town was bulldozed and completely rebuilt. Despite the obvious need for hasty reconstruction, efforts were made to emulate the earlier Venetian grandeur, at least around the main public areas. To a great extent they succeeded, although pre-earthquake visitors might disagree. The central area especially, with its ambient squares, arcaded streets and public buildings, rebuilt with a touch of the neo-classical and Venetian influence, is quite attractive. All building specifications since the 1953 earthquake, have to withstand well over 8 on the Richter Scale.

Earthquakes have always been a problem in this part of the world. One reason why Zakynthos has little to show of the Byzantine influence is the result of earthquakes during the seventeenth century. Damage was even inflicted in the nineteenth century which resulted in some rebuilding. In fact, between August 1953 and April 1954 a further 3,000 tremors were recorded. Minor tremors are a fact of every day life but mostly go unremarked by visitors unused to such phenomena.

Photographs of pre- and post-earthquake Zakynthos are displayed in the Library off Solomos Square. Lining the staircase are photographs of old Zakynthos whilst in a room upstairs there are some of post-earthquake Zakynthos and one showing the town ablaze.

Zakynthos Town

Below; Left & right: Fishing, Zakynthos Town

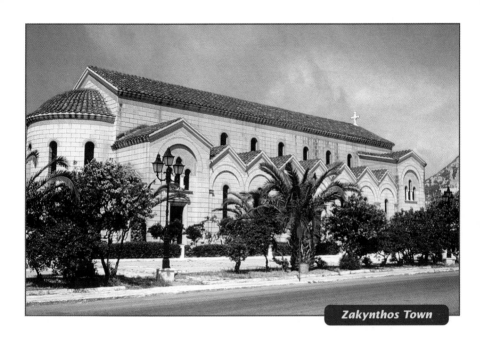

Zakynthos Town

Zakynthos Town

The Ionian islanders were just about picking up the threads of their lives again when the earthquake of 1953 struck.

Old commercial interests have faded and the island has a new paymaster, tourism, which is restoring some of its former purpose and prosperity. This is reflected in the quality of goods available in the shops which are as much for the home market as for tourist consumption. Horse-drawn carriages, less ornate than those of their Corfiot neighbours, drive visitors around the town on sightseeing tours whilst, for the more energetic, there are canopied dual cycles.

Solomos Square provides the pivot for access to the main points of interest and is situated close to most of the town's accommodation. After union with Greece, the square became known as King George I Square but is now named for Zakynthos' most famous poet, Dionysios Solomos (1798-1857). See box p42. Evenings are the time when this area comes alive, with the locals out for a volta (stroll). Edged by graceful arcaded buildings, small gardens, seats and an outdoor café, this large airy square is an ideal location to observe a touch of local colour.

Further along the coast to the north is located the NTOG (National Tourist Organisation of Greece) run pay beach. Not much in the way of a beach, more a place to swim, with showers, changing facilities, children's playground and a café. Boats for the various trips also leave from the quay at the north end whilst ferries dock down to the south near Ag Dionysios church.

The Church of St Nicholas on the Mole (Ag Nikolaos tou Molou) stands on the seaward edge of Solomos Square. The epithet 'Mole' derives from when the area now known as Solomos Square was called Molos. Founded in 1561, the church was built on an offshore islet and belonged to the local guild of seamen whose patron saint was St Nicholas. Besides service as a church, its bell-tower was used as a lighthouse at one time. It became part of the mainland when infill was used for development of the harbour. When the patron saint of the island, Dionysios, came from Aegina, he served as parish priest here for a while. A single-aisled basilica design, St Nicholas' was the only Venetian church in town to survive the 1953 fire. Since then it has been restored, at least externally. On Good Friday afternoon, the epitaphios (Christ's funeral bier) is taken in procession around the town from this church.

Next to the Church of St Nicholas, in Solomos Square, is the **Cultural Centre**. During the summer months, a pleasant outdoor café operates in the area nearest the church. The building houses the Municipal Library, which contains a display of miniature dolls wearing local costumes and a photographic record of Zakynthos. Visitors are free to wander in during the week when the library is open. This is also where the historical archives of Zakynthos are kept, at least those which were saved from the fire of 1953. In the same building can be found the 'Foscolo' cinema and the civic hall which is used for dances and theatrical performances. The latter replaced the destroyed neoclassical 'Foscolo' Municipal Theatre, designed by Ernst Ziller. Like Solomos, Hugo Foscolo (1778-

1827) was a famous son of the island whose statue stands outside the Town Hall on the southern side of the square. He was of Greek/Italian origin and found fame as a national poet of Italy.

Museum of Byzantine Art

At the back of the square is the **Museum of Byzantine Art**. This is the place to see a rich array of well displayed artistic treasures, especially the development in painting which took place in the two hundred years up to and including the nineteenth century. A model of pre-earthquake Zakynthos, on the ground floor, gives some impression of its previous Venetian style. Many of the exhibits are from churches around the island which were destroyed by earthquake. Brilliantly carved and painted ikonostases, ecclesiastical paintings and portable ikons, some in delicately worked silver, make up the bulk of the exhibits. A reconstruction of the interior of the Church of St Andrew (Ag Andreas Volimon), Volimes, brilliantly displays its superb seventeenth century frescos. There is also one room with a small collection of Hellenistic and Byzantine sculpted marble fragments. Open: Tues-Sun 8am-2.30pm; closed Monday. Admission charge.

From Solomos Square head inland to **St Mark's Square** (Ag Markou Platia), known as '*Platyforos*' by the locals. The life of the town has long revolved around this intimate square which was a gathering place for the nobility. Today, a combination of restaurant tables, spilling out onto the square, and souvenir shops create a lively ambience, especially in the evening. Here are located more buildings connected to Zakynthos' heritage. The Roman Catholic church of St Mark was founded in 1518 and still serves a large Catholic population, a leftover from Venetian times. It has undergone a series of reconstruction programmes since then and was rebuilt during the 1960s after destruction in 1953. Unfortunately, the interior is a shadow of its former glory as very few of its treasures have survived.

Next door to St Mark's church is the **Solomos Museum**. The ground floor contains the tombs of both Dionysios Solomos and another great Zakynthian poet Andreas Kalvos (1792-1869). Kalvos lived in Lincolnshire, England with his English wife, where he died. His remains were returned to Zakynthos in 1960. The museum is really only of interest to curious non-Greeks or those who can read Greek. It consists of a collection of memorabilia, manuscripts and personal effects etc of Solomos and other Zakynthian men of letters. Entry is free.

Leave St Mark's Square in a southerly direction along 21 Maiou which becomes the main arcaded shopping street of **Alexandrou Roma**. This has been the main street (Megali Rouga) and commercial

Continued on page 45...

• DIONYSIOS SOLOMOS (1798-1857) •

The ancestors of Dionysios Solomos arrived on Zakynthos from Crete, when the Turks wrested that island from the Venetians during the sixteenth century. Educated in Italy, he studied Italian, French and English literature. His first poetry was written in Italian but Greek Independence fervour inspired a switch to Greek, although he was never to visit independent Greece. He lived in the family mansion on Strani Hill, north of the castle, and a bust of the poet now marks the spot near there where he is reputed to have written 'A Hymn to Freedom' (c1823). Part of this poem was later set to music by the Corfiot composer Nikolaos Mantzaros (1795-1874) and became the Greek national anthem in 1864. A poem which became perhaps one of his greatest, 'The Free Besieged', was inspired by the sound of cannon fire during the siege of Messolongi, which could be heard on Zakynthos.

He is revered both as a Greek national poet and the first poet to write in 'demotic' Greek, the written form of the ordinary language. The language of the people against the language of officialdom, *'katharevousa'*, a version of ancient Greek regarded as the 'pure' language. Both these persisted in conflict until 1974, when *'dimotiki'* was officially adopted as the national language. This is the reason why there are so many conflicting spellings to be found of the same word.

His move to Corfu in 1828 stimulated cultural expansion there, as his crusade for the use of 'demotic' Greek as a recognised poetic medium gathered momentum. This culminated in the formation of the Corfu Literary School which insisted on the use of the modern language.

Solomos died on Corfu in 1857 and his body transferred back to Zakynthos ten years later. His home in Corfu town is also a museum dedicated to his memory.

Market. Zakynthos Town

Below; Left: Solomos Square Right: St Nicholas on the Mole

43

• SAINT DIONYSIOS •

Dionysios came from the noble family of Sigouri and was born sometime in the latter half of the sixteenth century. He started monastic life in the monastery on the isolated Strophades islands, which lie about 30 miles (48km) south of Zakynthos.

Stopping over in Athens, en route to the Holy Land, he was ordained Bishop of Aegina. A sick man, he returned to his native Zakynthos and spent the last years of his life in Anafonitria Monastery where he died on 17 December 1624. He was buried on the Strophades islands but his body was returned to Zakynthos on 24 August 1716. Remembered mainly for his charitable works, these two dates are celebrated in his memory and his remains carried in ceremonial procession around the town.

Believers claim he walks the island performing miracles and generally protecting Zakynthos. To compound this belief, his casket is opened each year and his feet fitted with a new pair of slippers. A carnival atmosphere accompanies the celebration of his saint's days with music, dancing and fireworks.

centre of the town since its founding in the 1500s. On the left, soon after leaving St Mark's Square, is a selection of reasonably priced fast food outlets where a constant stream of snackers ensures that produce is fresh. A goodly number of shops line both sides of the street and spill over into nearby side streets. Amongst the choices are a surprising number of upmarket outlets with correspondingly high prices. These are frequented as much by locals as tourists. On the other hand, there are plenty of shops catering for general tourist needs. Further away from St Mark's Square, the shops become more a window into the everyday life of the ordinary Greeks.

On the right, as the street becomes Alexandrou Roma, stands the Prefecture, which is the island's administrative centre. The street behind, Argassari, leads up to an old fountain and beyond, along Sartzadha, the church of the Virgin Pikridiotissa (Panagia Pikridiotissa). Its bell-tower is a dominant landmark on the hillside beneath the castle, which can be reached along a paved path from the church.

Out towards Alikes on the edge of town lies the **church of St Lazarus,** who was patron saint of the guild of shoemakers and tanners. The church, founded in 1500, started life as a monastery and is where St Gerassimos of Kefalonia served time as a curate. Another church of note, **Faneromeni,** is located close to Ag Dionysios. As opposed to St Mark's Square and its association with the nobility, the square by this church was the meeting place for the ordinary people of the town.

At the southern end of the harbour lie the monastery and **church of the island's patron saint, Dionysios**. Its bell-tower is a copy of that in St Mark's Square, Venice and dominates the waterfront view for those arriving by ferry. The monastery houses a small ecclesiastical museum but the church is the centre of attention. Of modern construction, it survived the 1953 earthquake and fire. The ornate interior of the three-aisled basilica has a richly painted ceiling, an intricately carved ikonostasis and a wealth of gold and silver decoration where the double-headed Byzantine eagle figures strongly. Amidst this show of wealth, in a side chapel to the right of the altar, lie the remains of St Dionysios himself encased within a large silver casket. These are removed on the days of the saint's festivals and paraded round the town in a glass-fronted gilt casket. The church is open 4am-12noon and 5-9pm.

Return back along the harbour front, **Strata Marina**, to Solomos Square. Along here is where the warehouses used to be located which stored the islands major export, raisins. Today, it is where to find tourist and shipping agencies.

The castle is approached by following the road up the hill to Tsilivi. Turn left for Bochali and the Kastro on reaching the cross-roads at the top of the hill. Bochali Square is reached with the sixteenth century church of Our Lady of Chrysopigi (golden spring), restaurants and cafés. From the terrace here there is a magnificent view over the town and to the Peloponnese beyond. Continue up to enter the outer gate, with a Venetian lion plaque above, and two further inner gates to the huge hilltop area which once enclosed the medieval town. Apart from a few remnants, earthquakes and neglect have taken their toll on the many buildings which once crowded inside the existing walls, which included around twelve churches. Pine trees, planted in their place, now provide a sheltered arbour for summer picnics. A magnificent panoramic view can be enjoyed from the highest point of the walls over most of the island.

This is the probable site of ancient Psophis but earthquakes down the centuries have obliterated any traces of its Cyclopean walls. Finds have been unearthed here as they have at Bochali cemetery close by. This second site is believed to have been an ancient stadium and is where the Venetians held horse races and public assemblies. Temples to Apollo and Aphrodite are also thought to have once stood in the vicinity.

PART 3: Car Tours

All the car tours which follow elect Zakynthos town as the starting point although few people actually use it as a base. Joining the tour at some convenient point should present no great difficulty from any other resort since all of them lie fairly close to Zakynthos town.

CAR TOUR I:
SOUTHERN ZAKYNTHOS

This excursion tours two of the islands major resorts and some of its most popular beaches so be sure to pack a swimming costume. Just about every stop along the way provides opportunities for dining but those with a picnic in mind might think of Banana Beach or Gerakas Beach. Allow a full day for the tour, not that the driving takes too much time for the total distance covered is only around 37.5 miles (60km), for there is plenty to see and do. The full itinerary includes Laganas, Kalamki, Argassi, Kaminia Beach, Porto Zoro, Banana Beach, Plaka Beach, Ag Nikolaos Beach, Porto Roma and Gerakas before returning to Zakynthos town.

The road out to Laganas leaves Zakynthos from the south end of the promenade and, once out of town, it is a fast road. There is a left turn to enter the long approach down to the beach. Do not be disturbed by a sign apparently announcing Pandokratoras which merely indicates the parish boundary within which Laganas falls. Notice the major road to Kalamaki on the left shortly before the beach is reached. For parking, keep ahead down High Street to the parking area on the beach.

Laganas, surrounded by olive groves, is surprisingly spread out for a major resort. Tourist shops, restaurants, bars and tavernas add colour and enliven the approach road to the beach as they do along the Kalamaki road. While there are some large hotels, generally low buildings and a low density of building lend a spacious feel to the resort, especially since there are still plenty of trees around. Restaurants, tavernas and fast food outlets cater for just about every taste, full English breakfast is served all day here and there are plenty of take-aways including traditional fish and chips English style. If a restaurant is preferred it is possible to eat Chinese, Indian, Italian, vegetarian and even Greek! Night owls have plenty of choice too in Laganas when the bars swing into action during the evening and there is a choice of discos.

It might seem hard to believe but as recently as 1982 there was only a bakery and a few houses along High Street and a couple of bars along the beach. Some of the old postcards on sale still show the town this way. But the beach is very different now. It is a long beach ribboning along the whole of Lagana Bay, from Laganas all the way to Kalamaki, the adjoining resort. A full 3.75 miles (6km) long, it is claimed to be one of the longest beaches in Greece. Bars and tavernas lie shoulder to shoulder on the beach offering food and cooling drinks while in front are rows of sun beds and umbrellas, usually towards the back of the beach. A gently shelving beach and shallow seas make it a good resort for families. Strollers will find the compact sand easy to walk on and those heading for the quieter southern end will find a small fishermen's harbour. From here a coastal footpath continues to a small, peaceful beach known as Ag Sostis, but not too quiet since it has bars and restaurants. There is supposedly a ban on speedboats in Lagana Bay to protect the loggerhead turtles but its introduction was not generally welcomed. The islanders have something of a dichotomous view on the loggerhead turtles, in the main they are proud that they live in these waters and breed on the island's beaches but when their presence stops them making money, attitudes change. Some water sports are in action with pedaloes and canoes available for hire and organised boat trips on offer, especially to see the loggerhead turtles; sightings guaranteed is the usual claim.

Normally, the Greeks are laid back about life and making money, generally waiting for business to find them. Zakynthos Greeks are different in this respect, they actually look for business. Just outside town lies Sarakina restaurant which offers a good Greek cuisine with entertainment by Greek folk dancers. To make sure of custom, a free minibus is laid on from the town centre. Dennis' taverna at Lithakia, another out of town restaurant which offers the most authentic Greek food in town and the best prices, also lays on free transport and similarly lays on Greek dancing to entertain guests.

Sarakini

Sarakini restaurant takes its name from the Venetian mansion which belonged to the Sarakini family. Although seriously damaged by the earthquake and overgrown with shrubs and trees, the mansion still stands and it is a pleasant 30 minute walk out to view it. If time is short, it is possible to drive and just walk the last 5 minutes. On leaving the beach, head inland along High Street and take the road on the left, just past the road off right to Kalamki. The road quickly leads into the olive groves and around here are some of the most attractive groves on the island with old trees gnarled and twisted into wonderful shapes. (see feature on page 49).

Leave Laganas by taking the road to Kalamaki which is rapidly developing into a smaller version of Laganas. Turn right at the far end to head down to Kalamaki beach.

Typical of many resorts in the Ionian islands, **Kalamaki** has no

Continued on page 52...

• THE OLIVE •

Known from Crete as early as 3,500BC, the olive has been central to the existence of the Mediterranean peoples for millennia. Although grown primarily for oil for cooking, the oil is also used as a lubricant, for lighting, soap making and in ointments and liniments for the skin. The fruit itself, the olive, is also eaten.

The tree is evergreen with leathery lance-shaped leaves which are dark green above and silvery beneath. With age the trunks become gnarled and twisted adding considerably to the character of the tree. It takes 4-8 years for a tree to start bearing fruit but full production is not reached until after 15-20 years and it may then continue for centuries with proper care. The tree is erratic in that not every year produces a good crop, unless a suitable regime of irrigation and feeding is rigorously followed, but more often good crops are expected every other year. Whitish flowers borne in loose clusters arrive in late spring which rely on the wind for pollination. The fruit which follows takes 6-8 months to reach full maturity for only then does it give the maximum yield of oil. This means that harvesting takes place throughout the winter months, from December through until March, the perfect complement to working in the tourist season. Fruits for eating are collected before maturity and need special treatment with dilute caustic lye and salt to kill the extreme bitterness. There are hundreds of named varieties of olives, both for oil and for eating, which are propagated from hardwood cuttings or from leaf cuttings under mist propagation.

Olive oil is produced in a selection of grades, the very finest oil from the first pressing is known as virgin oil and this is the grade preferred for salad dressing. It is a good buy to take home too and can be found on supermarket shelves in 1 or 5 litre containers. The second grade of oil is the pure, a blend of virgin oil, and refined oil is the third grade. Refined oil is made from the *lampante* grade, so called because it is used for lamp fuel, by treatment to remove the acid, the colour and the odour. *Lampante* is obtained from a second pressing of the residual pulp.

The wood too is of great value. It is very hard, strongly grained and takes a fine polish, ideal for carving, cabinet work and toys. It is good too as a slow burning fuel and for making charcoal for which the Greeks have a great demand.

Botanically, the olive, *Olea europea*, belongs to the Oleaceae family and has some interesting and familiar relatives like ash, privet, jasmine and lilac.

Relaxing on the beach, Laganas

Below; Left: The church of Ag. Lypios is perched on the hillside near Zakynthos Town Right: Argassi Church

Argassi

Porto Roma

focal point and development simply spreads along the roadside. The beach is of fine, dark sand similar to Laganas beach and again it is lapped by a shallow sea but the main difference is that there is barely any commercialisation as yet. Crystal Beach Hotel backs onto the beach and offers taverna and bar facilities and a swimming pool open to all. Again, the restriction on the use of motor boats in this bay reduces the water sports on offer. This end of the beach is used by the turtles in the breeding season and consequently it is off limits at night time. Kalamaki offers a good beach, a smaller resort than Laganas but close enough to take advantage of its facilities and is only 3.1 miles (5km) from Zakynthos town. There is also the possibility of walking over the hills to reach Argassi.

Apart from enjoying the beach, there is little to detain the casual visitor so from here it is a question of heading inland back towards Zakynthos town keeping close to a range of hills on the right. There is a cut through towards Argassi without the need to go back into Zakynthos town but before this is reached, look on the hillside for the blue and white church of Ag Lypios with its typical Zakynthian bell tower. Shortly afterwards, a right turn leads onto the northern coast road of the Gerakas peninsula and Argassi is then soon reached.

Argassi, just 1.9 miles (3km) outside Zakynthos town, straggles along the main road which runs parallel but slightly inland from the coast at this point. Some developments also lie alongside the road running inland. Smaller than Laganas, it is another cosmopolitan

resort with something for everybody. Fast foods are available as well as a selection of restaurants and tavernas and when the sun sets there is a good choice of bars and discos to stretch the evening well into the night.

When beaches were dealt out around the island, Argassi did not fare too well. It has a long, narrow strip of dark sand which is stony in parts and affected by sea weed in others. It looks better when colourfully decked with beach beds, umbrellas and sun bathers. To the west end is a curious three-arched bridge which now runs into the sea. It bears the date 1886 but is probably earlier since it is referred to as Venetian and was originally carrying part of a coastal road. There are plenty of facilities to hand and it is not necessary to stir far to find a glass of cold beer. A good range of water sports is available too which are confined to one area for the general safety of bathers.

Driving south-east, the rest of the peninsula offers some of the island's finest beaches which are all signposted. It is a pleasant run along the wooded peninsula to **Kaminia**, the first stop. This is a fairly new development around a small beach with a beach bar, restaurants and sunbeds.

Neighbouring **Porto Zoro** is an unspoilt beach of fine golden sand set in a small bay in natural surroundings. Backed by low hills, it is bounded by a headland to the west and lent additional character by the short spit which leads out to a jumble of huge rocks at the other end of the bay. Thatched sun shades add their own exotic touch to this inviting beach. Some water sports are available including jet skis, motor boats, pedaloes and canoes whilst a beach-side taverna is on hand to dispense cool drinks and feed the hungry.

Next beach along is **Banana Beach**, accessed along a woodland track, just after Ano Vasilikos. This leads down to a small parking area and from there it is a short walk down to around the centre of the beach. Banana Beach is as beautiful and natural as any on the island. A long ribbon of fine golden sand traces the shoreline outwards around a curving headland in something of a banana shape. Sun bathers seek shade from the sun under the rich brown thatch of the parasols when not swimming or dashing about on jet skis or using the other water sport facilities. Out of the main season, expect this beach to be very quiet and it is unlikely that the tavernas and the beach bars will all be fully operational before early June. Similarly, the full gamut of water sports is not operational until high season.

• CARETTA CARETTA, THE LOGGERHEAD TURTLE •

The sandy beaches of Zakynthos have for millions of years been the breeding ground of the loggerhead turtle. Unfortunately, the recent growth of tourism on the island is threatening these traditional breeding grounds and their continued existence in this part of the Mediterranean. Essentially warm water animals, they live also in the Atlantic, the Black Sea, the Pacific and Indian oceans.

The breeding season starts in early June when the adult female turtles head towards the beaches in late afternoon at the risk these days of being cut to pieces from jet skis and motorboats. It is their size which makes them so vulnerable, they can exceed a 3ft 3in (1m) in length and weigh something in the region of 220lbs (100kg) On reaching their favoured beach, assuming that there are no lights or noises hinting at danger, they haul themselves ashore and lay up to 100 eggs in a clutch beneath the warm sands.

Incubation takes around two months and, provided that they have survived the trample of feet and the danger of being pierced by the poles of sun shades, they hatch into miniature turtles faced with the task of reaching the sea for their continued survival. This is a time in their life cycle when they are at their most vulnerable from natural predators.

The breeding season as a whole lasts from June to September, just about coinciding with the tourist season but there are a number of ways in which visitors can help. Avoid the nesting beaches at night, do not dig in the soft sands, avoid using umbrellas which need to be staked into the sand, use no lights, make no noise at nights and shun activities which rely on the use of speed boats in the areas where the turtles are known to breed.

Ag. Nikolaos

Plaka Beach, next along this road, is nothing more than a small intimate, sandy cove with a taverna. A neat lawn behind extends the relaxing area for pitching sunbeds. Between Plaka and Banana Beaches, beneath the Golden Bay Village, is another bay full of rocky shelves and sandy coves.

A stone's throw further south lies lively **Ag. Nikolaos**. A water sports centre awaits the active and a noisy beach bar gives plenty of atmosphere. A play area is provided for children with a nearby lawn for relaxing parents. The south end of the beach with its Greek taverna offers a quiet escape.

Porto Roma, the next destination a little further down the peninsula, is a peaceful backwater. There is a small harbour with fishing boats and a very narrow stretch of dark sand with a sprinkling of shingle which makes up the beach. The greatest delight to Porto Roma is the fish taverna of the same name which overlooks the harbour and offers a

dining opportunity which attracts the Greeks themselves, always a good recommendation.

The final port of call on this tour lies at the very end of the peninsula, Gerakas Beach.

Beautiful **Gerakas Beach** is one of the favoured haunts of the loggerhead turtle, *Caretta caretta*, (see feature p53) which has effectively limited development. The beach itself is a graceful arc of fine golden sand filling the extensive bay and backed by low cliffs. With the sands shelving only gently into the sea, it is an ideal beach for families. Sun beds and umbrellas are available for hire but bars and tavernas are not allowed on the beach and are to be found close by on the approach road. Access to the beach is prohibited after sunset to protect the turtles and this is strictly enforced and policed in the breeding season.

A ride back along the peninsula to Zakynthos town completes this tour.

CAR TOUR 2: THE RIZA ROAD

Zakynthos is neatly divided into the mountainous west and the fertile east. A line of farming villages mark the division and the route of this tour follows the road along the foot of the mountains known as the Riza Road which links them all together like a string of pearls ending in Alikes. The return follows through Alikanas and then roughly along the coast catching a beach or two before reaching the growing resort of Tsilivi. Set aside a full day for this short tour of around 40 miles (64km) if one or two of the villages are to be explored and the beaches put to good use. Not all the villages are worth a stop, the earthquake of 1953 robbed them of their old character, but the countryside offers a sharp contrast in scenery between the hills on one side and the fertile plain on the other. Starting from Zakynthos town, the route takes in Pandokratoras, Macherado, Katastari, Alikes, Alikanas, Ano Gerakari, Planos, Tsilivi and back to Zakynthos town.

Ag. Marina

Use the fast road out of Zakynthos town towards Laganas but keep straight ahead at the Laganas junction heading towards Lithakia but keep an eye open shortly for the left turn into **Pandokratoras** (Pantokratoras). This is the administrative centre of the parish which includes Laganas and is quite a large village. The road passes beneath so there is not too much to see without stopping to explore and then interest is mainly confined to its two churches, Ag Nikolaos built in 1815 and the church of Our Lady from which the village takes its name. Pandokratoras almost runs into the next village of Mouzaki and from there picturesque Romiri is quickly reached followed by Macherado.

Macherado, which takes its name from the Machairas family, is a major village and stopping point on round-the-island tours and other excursions. Ag. Mavra church built in 1873 is the pride of the village and the focus of interest for visitors. It belongs to the Tavarias family and is dedicated to two Egyptian saints, Mavra and Timotheos, who were martyred in the third century AD. Apart from the impressive free-standing square bell tower, the exterior of the church is plain in sharp contrast to the highly decorative single-isled interior. It has become the custom to lock churches with valued possessions these days but this one is usually kept open with a custodian in attendance. First to catch the eye is the huge ikon of Agia Mavra on a gilded throne of carved wood which is surrounded by scenes from her miracles and martyrdom and often hung with votive offerings. The theme of elaborate wood carv-

ing continues in the gilded ikonostasis and again in the elaborately carved pulpit. Equally ornate is the painted ceiling which shows Mathew, Mark Luke and John surrounded by scenes including Adam and Eve and the story of Moses.

The onward route continues to cut across the island passing close to small villages which lie on the hillside just off the main road.

Ag Marina is worth a stop, not necessarily for its church with an interesting onion-domed bell-tower, but for Taverna Parthenon which lies in the hills almost immediately above the village. Just follow signs to Dennis' place. This is a great spot to drink in the views from its elevated terrace over a lunch of old Zakynthian style food for which the taverna is famed or simply taking refreshments. It overlooks the area of fertile plain which is the engine of the islands economy producing olive oil, grapes, citrus fruit and raisins.

Moving on, the next village, **Skoulikado**, is known on the island for its strong tradition in music but otherwise has little of interest. From here there are a few more hamlets en route, and a chance to fill up with petrol at Pigadakia, before the Riza road eventually runs out at Karastari. Turn right here for Alikes, then left.

Alikes is a great place for relaxing, developed enough to provide a good choice in facilities but still on the quiet side. The beach of soft, silver sand fills a wide sweep of bay and is divided into three sections by two small jetties. With few buildings encroaching onto the rear and the main road lying a little inland, the beach is natural and unspoilt. Facili-

• RAISINS AND ROOFS •

Raisins, introduced by the Peloponnesians who settled on the island during the Venetian years, were once a major crop and important source of revenue. The raisin grape was grown extensively on the plain and any other fertile corner of the island which would support them. Many houses and villages had threshing floors which also served as an area to spread and dry the grapes. So lucrative and important was this trade to the island that raisin smuggling carried a death penalty. It continued up to World War II but loss of outlets diminished the trade and their markets were taken over by new producers.

Roofs here refers to the thatched roofed structures on stilts often seen in fields, called *kaleva*. These often rickety looking constructions are raised away from the heat of the land to benefit from cooling breezes. Their main purpose was to provide a shaded resting area for farmers working in the fields. So effective were these structures for keeping cool that their popularity spread and they were often built in gardens and on house rooftops for overnight sleeping, although modern versions are sometimes characterless prefabricated structures. Some are also used on the sea shore as inexpensive beach houses.

ties are close to hand, all the usual beach furniture is available for hire and there is a full range of water sports. A river enters the sea on the eastern side of the resort and there is yet more beach beyond, reached by a footbridge over the river. Some tour operators sell this eastern part as Alikanas in their package holidays but this lies a short way away from here and is visited shortly.

From here the tour now heads back towards Zakynthos town following the coast. The village of Alikanas, just 1.9 miles (3km) away, is soon reached.

Alikanas is developing as a resort around an existing village which is

Cycle round Alikes

Bicycle hire is popular in Alikes and, with areas around which are not too hilly, there is scope for some gentle rides. A bike is handy for exploring the nearby disused salinas which were once active in the production of salt from sea water but now provide a football pitch. There is a good choice of eating places in town and the food prices are generally better value here than in the more major resorts of Laganas and Argassi. Cocktail bars and discos provide the evening entertainment.

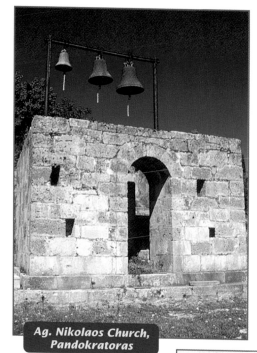

Ag. Nikolaos Church, Pandokratoras

Ag. Marina

a little unusual for this island. Some purpose-built apartments are springing up in the countryside around the village but development is still low key and the facilities are still minimal. It is a great place for a quiet holiday although there may be some walking involved to reach a beach. There are beaches either side of the village. The easiest access is to Ag Kiriaki beach on the Alikes side where there is also a small fishing harbour but Alikanas beach, sometimes called Xehoriate, lies on the other side of the village. This beach, reached by descending from the main road, has a ribbon of fine, silver sand in totally natural surroundings although some

Alikanes beach

development has taken place on the headland just to the north. Sun loungers and parasols are available with a bar handy to keep refreshments flowing.

Continuing beyond Alikanas, there is another small sandy cove at **Ammoudi** with some beach facilities including a bar. Keeping along the coast road, there is a succession of small beaches to discover. **Drossia** offers a small strip of sandy beach with a café while **Porto Rouli** has an inviting beach-side taverna overlooking a small strip of sand and, further along the coast road, an old Venetian watch tower. Last in this succession is **Amboula**. The presence of the hotel ensures a supply of tavernas around this small beach of fine sand which is provided with a shower as well as other creature comforts in the way of bars and beach furniture.

From here the coast road runs all the way back to Zakynthos town but there are two stops to make at Planos and Tsilivi which are probably close enough to eventually merge. **Planos** has a long, narrow beach but **Tsilivi** has some 1.6 miles (2.5km) of fine golden sands which terminate in a small harbour to the left. The sea is shallow here and the beach has easy access which makes it ideal for families. Bars and tavernas are scattered around lightly enough to preserve the natural ambience. Plenty of water sports are on offer and the beach is well supplied with sun beds and umbrellas. Much of the development has taken place along the main road which runs just a little inland where there is a comprehensive selection of tavernas offering international cuisine including Chinese and English. Night life is developing steadily and already the choice includes cocktail or music bars, a disco, night-club, karaoke bar and for those who prefer a traditional pint, an English style pub.

CAR TOUR 3: THE HIGH ROAD

A completely different perspective of the island can be enjoyed on this tour. The route first penetrates the southernmost reaches of the island before heading up the island along an exhilarating high road to the north. Tiny coves beneath towering cliffs are enticing and mainly inaccessible but the views are fantastic. Enjoy a wander off the beaten track around sleepy villages like Agalas, Louka and Geri and admire the unusual bell-tower at Kiliomeno, Mycenaean rock tombs near Kambi and an old monastery at Anafonitria. See Car Tour 4 if wishing to include a visit to Smugglers Cove on this trip. The basic round trip from Zakynthos town is about 87.5 miles (140km) in distance.

Head out of Zakynthos town along the Laganas road, keeping ahead to Keri where the road goes off left to Laganas and the shore. Continue ahead at the cross-roads below Lithakia village. Up right through the village is the continuation of this tour and left leads past the Laganas camping ground to the beach at Ag Sostis. Pass the left turn off to Porto Koukla, which leads through a wonderful grove of medieval olive trees en route to a small beach, but turn left at the sign to **Limni Keriou** (Keri Lake). The area to the left, known as Keri Lake, is actually swamp and has been known as a source of bitumen since antiquity. It is possible to find traces of bitumen here today. **Keri Limni Beach** lies in a secluded bay opposite Marathonisi island. It is a relatively quiet location with low-key development, tavernas and shops. Sun beds are available on the narrow sloping beach, which is a mix of stone, sand and shingle with a shading of tamarisk trees in part,

and there is a diving centre. Regular boat trips leave from the small harbour to view Keri Caves and out to Marathonis Island. The beach on the island is supposedly out of bounds as it is a turtle breeding area.

Continuing south through a verdant cloak of olive and pine trees, the village of **Keri**, nestling on the hillside out of view of the sea, is soon reached. Park here for exploring the village as the road narrows to enter the tiny square where there are cafés. In the valley bottom below the village sits the renovated church of the Virgin Keriotissa with its stumpy bell-tower, easy to access on foot from the village but the road to it is quite a way back down the main road towards Laganas. Ultimately, to reach the end of the road, take the narrow road right just before the village square, signposted to **Faros Keriou** (Keri Lighthouse) which lies a little under 1.25 miles (2km) away. The road reverts to rough track on the final rise to the Lighthouse on the cliff edge. Those unwilling to risk driving their car or moped further, can park here and walk the short distance up to the lighthouse for wonderful cliff-top views.

Retrace the outward route back as far as Lithakia cross-roads and turn left. Dennis' Taverna on a corner of the cross-roads here is a great place for genuine Greek food. Lithakia is one of the oldest villages on the island but earthquake damage has erased much of its older buildings of note. The road winds up through the village and past quarrying to a left turn to the small rural settlement of Agalas. Close by is the unusual two-tier cave of Domianou.

Back on the main road, rise up to reach the village of **Kiliomeno**. This village was formerly known by the name of its church, St Nicholas, its intriguing wedding cake style bell-tower and traditional two-storey houses making it worth a stop. Turn up left in the village centre. Right leads down to Macherado along a very scenic road. The onward road along this high level route is good and very scenic. Shortly before reaching Ag Leon, a road is signposted off right to the villages of **Louka** and **Geri** whose early inhabitants included immigrants from the Mani area of the Peloponnese. The villages lie tucked into fertile folds of the barren hillsides. They suffered less earthquake damage in 1953 than the rest of the island so consequently are a microcosm of an old way of life, except that the population has dwindled to a few remaining inhabitants. At least they are worth a detour off the main road.

Ag. Leon uses the base of a disused windmill for its bell-tower and spreads either side of the main road. On the approach to Exo Hora, turn left for Kambi. The white cross on the cliff-top is the ultimate destination at **Skiza**. Fork left in the village of Kambi, then turn right at the T-junction. Pass a taverna and continue uphill, looking for the sign on the left which marks the site of rock-cut Mycenaean tombs reached by a short path. Beneath the towering cross, erected to commemorate those who lost their lives during the Greek Civil War in the late 1940s, is the Cross Taverna. The name might not be imaginative but the location is superb and the food good and reasonable. An ideal spot to watch the sun go down whilst enjoying a meal or a drink.

Go left at the main road into **Exo Hora** where some pre-earthquake houses still stand. Further along the road reach **Maries**, in the vicinity of which has been located another Mycenaean cemetery. As the road comes to a T-Junction, where right continues on to Volimes, turn left towards **Anafonitria**. The village, with its large plane tree-shaded *platia*, lies a little to the right, but keep ahead to the monastery which lies close to where the road goes off left down to Porto Vromi. To give it its full title, the fifteenth century Monastery of the Virgin Anafonitria is where the island's patron saint Dionysios spent the last years of his life. The original medieval tower still stands at the entrance, its fortifications now serving a more peaceful purpose as a bell-tower. A vaulted archway leads to a courtyard and the church which is the island's oldest three-aisled basilica. St Dionysios' cell is still there and

Kiliomeno

contains ikons and vestments
which were used by the saint himself. Another thought provoking
chapel within the monastery walls
is dedicated to St Anastasia the
Dissolver of Poisons!

Descend to cross the plain to return directly to Zakynthos town
through **Katastari**, the largest village on the island. A modern
double-fronted church dominates
the village square which houses
many works of art from other,
now ruined, churches in the area. At
the next village of **Ag Dimitrios**,
traces of an ancient temple to
Artemis have been found. Unfortunately, as with other finds on
Zakynthos, the tantalising remnants
of its ancient past have been all
but obliterated. This makes it even
more difficult to build up a clear
picture of life here in ancient times.
Once through attractive Ag Kyrikos,
Zakynthos town is soon reached.

Kiliomeno

CAR TOUR 4: SMUGGLERS COVE AND THE NORTHERN TIP

Smugglers Cove is offered as a boat trip but the most dramatic views of the cove with the shipwrecked boat are from the cliffs above. A road now speeds visitors to this fine viewpoint passing St George's monastery along the way. Fine mountain scenery abounds at the northern end of the island where this tour penetrates to reach the picturesque port of Ag Nikolaos. Allow a full day for this itinerary which requires around 75 miles (120km) of driving and includes Zakynthos town, Lithakia, Anafonitria, Smugglers Cove, Volimes, Ag Nikolaos, Ano Volimes before returning to Zakynthos via Katastari. The Callinico wine factory lies on the return leg so there is the option to drop in for a quick tasting session.

Smugglers Cove

There is a choice of route to reach Anafonitria which is effectively the starting point of this tour but the one chosen is both fast and scenic. Leave Zakynthos town heading towards Lithakia and follow signs to Kiliomeno. The road rises from Lithakia onto the hilltops through a long gorge which is scarred somewhat by quarries. Details of this section of the journey are included in Car Tour 3 as are details of Anafonitria itself.

On reaching the outskirts of Anafonitria, ignore the dominant signs to Smugglers Cove which point left. Following these signs leads down only to **Porto Vromi** where fishermen await to take visitors by boat. Go right to reach the village square with its huge plane tree and follow signs for St George's monastery. Shortly after passing the monastery, the road takes a sharp turn back left and then down to the viewpoint from where picture postcard views are obtained of the steel hull of a ship now half buried in sand. The ship was wrecked as recently as 1971 when it was supposedly smuggling tobacco and spirits. It took shelter here from a storm but was unluckily washed ashore to create a fascinating tourist attraction. People suffering from vertigo may be disturbed by the sheer cliffs here and children too should be kept to hand, alhough there is a railed, projecting platform for viewing.

From Anafonitria continue towards Volimes amidst the grandeur of some fine, if barren, mountain scenery. Roadside displays of kilims and lace announce arrival at **Volimes**. Volimes here is two villages rolled into one, it represents Meso (middle) Volimes and Kato (lower) Volimes while standing separately is Ano (upper) Volimes just along the Askos road. Wall-to-wall carpets and lace around the village are a result of encouraging the residents to form a Women's Agrotourism Co-operative in 1988. Now these villages are the centre of hand made lace and rugs on the island but there are also more traditional products like honey and cheese for sale. The parish church of Ag Paraskevi is worth a quick inspection if only for the finely carved and ornate stone around the doorway and windows.

Turn right in the village for the road to Ag Nikolaos and follow the narrow but good road which winds its way steadily down to the coast and the fishing village.

Ag Nikolaos is a small but picturesque fishing village and harbour with a small shingle beach. Apart from the beauty of its location, there is little to the village except a hotel, tavernas and a few tourist shops. As a destination on many of the organised round the island trips, it is overtly touristy and the prices correspondingly higher. The island's famous **Blue Caves** lie along the coast just north of Ag Nikolaos so there are usually boat trips on offer. It is also possible to drive up to **Cape Skinari** and see the water around the Blue Caves from land. While the incredible blueness of the water is still striking, it has not the same impact as sailing into the caves by boat.

Ferry boats large enough to take cars leave Ag Nikolaos daily for Kefalonia, a journey which takes about 1 hour 15 minutes. There is little point in making the crossing without a car or being part of an organised tour since the ferry docks at Pessada on Kefalonia which is nothing more than a remote landing stage. See the later section on excursions from the island for more details.

Leave Ag Nikolaos by the road which follows south along the coast and soon turn left towards Micro Nisi. Picturesque **Mikro Nisi** with its Venetian watch tower, sits on a projecting headland and, shortly afterwards, **Makris Gialos** is reached. Makris Gialos offers nothing more than an exquisite beach of fine shingle in totally natural surroundings. There is a café bar and a taverna to hand with sunbeds on the exposed beach.

Continue down the coast to meet the road from Anafonitria. Turn left here to Katastari and left again to Alikes. From here, follow the main road back towards Zakynthos town. As the main road divides approaching the village of Kalipado, use the bypass but look on the right here for the **Callinico Wine Factory**. Although wine is not manufactured until September and there is little to see until then, visitors are still invited to drop in and taste wine. Next there is a chance to try **go-kart racing** at the track near **Vanato** which is well signposted. An easy run from here back to Zakynthos town completes this tour.

• KOMBOLOI: TOYS FOR BOYS •

Usually a string of wooden, plastic or metal beads, *komboloi* are the Greek's own form of worry beads used by men to relax from the stresses and strains of everyday life. It seems to be a preserve of men and women are rarely seen using them. Partially wrapped around the fingers, the beads are revolved in a flicking motion but there are several techniques of worrying which are surprisingly difficult to imitate for the untrained. *Komboloi* are thought to have developed from the Turkish rosary which has 99 pearls representing the names of Allah. This is clearly too unwieldy to use as a toy so the Greeks reduced the number to 13 or 15, or sometimes 17. For the Greeks it is a toy or a lucky charm and has no religious significance whatsoever.

Out and About

PART 4: Excursions from the island

There are three very popular excursions off the island offered by tour operators; a day trip to Olympia, a two-day trip to the capital, Athens, and a day trip to Kefalonia. All these can be done independently if desired. Regular service KTEL buses run from Zakynthos to Athens which is perhaps the most economical way to travel but there are also daily flights. A privately organised trip to Olympia or Kefalonia would require a hire car and the economics are unfavourable unless the party size is at least four.

KEFALONIA

Kefalonia is a dramatically beautiful island with more than enough highlights to fill a day. It is an easy crossing by car from Ag Nikolaos on the northern tip of the island to Pessada, just south of Kefalonia's capital, Argostoli. The ferry crossing time is around 1 hour 15 minutes and a return ticket costs twice the price of a single journey which means that there is no additional ferry cost if an overnight stop on Kefalonia is planned. Argostoli itself is the best base for a short stop and there is plenty of accommodation but for a first try enquire at Vivian Villa (☎ 0671 23396, English spoken) which offers good apartments and rooms in a quiet but convenient location.

Organised tours have slightly different programmes on the island according to individual operators, some but not necessarily all of the following locations are usually included.

ARGOSTOLI

An interesting few hours can be filled by a visit to Argostoli. Sitting on the shores of an inner lagoon of the Gulf of Argostoli the views are inland to the mountains with one's back to the sea. A short taxi

ride or walk away are the lovely sandy beaches at Lassi with an abundance of water sports.

Argostoli has a spacious feel with a large central square surrounded by pavement cafés and oleander-lined streets, which are a riot of pink in summer. Late to tourism, the town still retains much of its Greekness and boasts a selection of good restaurants and tavernas. The people are friendly and most speak English so communication is not difficult. The town has a wide promenade and good waterfront atmosphere. Here, the fishermen sell their catch from boats and hourly ferries ply back and forth across the gulf to Lixouri, the second major town on the island. The waterfront, near the bus station, is where the excellent fruit and vegetable market is located. In the same area can also be found super-markets, bakeries, butchers and even a delicatessen. Pedestrianised Lithostroto, the oldest street in town, runs parallel with the shore south of the main square. This narrow street is the main tourist shopping area and is also where more upmarket boutiques can be found. Close to the main square is the Archaeological Museum, which houses a collection of mainly Mycenaean and Hellenistic finds from the island. An imaginatively displayed museum is the Korgialenios Historical and Folklore Museum, one of the best of its kind in Greece. This museum is located in the Korgialenios Library, reached by walking up the left side of the newly restored Kefalos Theatre, which lies up to the right on leaving the Archaeological Museum. Exhibits give a window onto nineteenth century life in Argostoli, which was amaz-

ingly sophisticated, with examples of exquisite lace work, and a whole array of artefacts all beautifully cared for and with explanations in English. Possibly the most poignant display, is a photographic record of pre-earthquake Argostoli and afterwards. A museum not to be missed.

LASSI

Close to Argostoli, this is the major tourist area on the island. It offers a number of fine sandy beaches which include Makrys Gialos and Platys Gialos where there are a full range of water sports.

ASSOS

Picturesque Assos has a romantic location on the narrow neck of a peninsula below a Venetian castle. Very photogenic and worth visiting to enjoy the ambience and, if time allows, to walk up to the castle.

FISKARDO

Important and picturesque fishing harbour on the northern tip of the island from where ferry boats leave for Lefkas and Ithaka. Fiskardo, with its pastel coloured neo-classical houses, survived the massive earthquake of 1953 and the village has now been declared a preservation area so all new construction must be in sympathy and retain the same architectural features.

Wandering south from the harbour area leads around the headland to a small shingle beach. On the way, the road passes close to excavations where a number of sarcophagi are on view from the Roman Period.

Ruins of an old Byzantine church lie on Fournios headland to the north and are easily reached on foot. There is thought to have been a church on this site since the sixth century but this present structure is much later and is remarkable for the two towers guarding the church entrance.

AG GERASSIMOS MONASTERY

Ag Gerassimos is the island's patron saint and this monastery is greatly revered by the islanders and draws pilgrims from all over Greece. The smaller chapel contains the remains of the saint in a silver casket standing near the ikonostasis and also within the chapel is a small cave where Gerassimos is said to have lived for a period on his arrival.

Ag Gerassimos is a fairly modern saint born in Trikala in Corinthia in 1507, son of a wealthy family. His ecclesiastical leanings were evident early in life when, in 1537, he went off to the Holy Land for 12 years and returned to take up Holy Orders. He settled in Zakynthos for a few years, living in a cave, before he came to Kefalonia and eventually settled in the Omala valley. Here, he took over an abandoned chapel to establish a nunnery and spent the remainder of his life tending the welfare of the villagers and their children. He died in 1579 and in the following years many miracles are claimed to have taken place. When his body was exhumed in 1581, it was found not to have decomposed and he was declared a saint.

SAMI

Sami is a popular resort area and port which attracts visitors for the two nearby caves, Drogarati and Melissani.

Drogarati cave is estimated to have developed over 150 million years although it was discovered only last century. As a commercial venture it has been open for some 30 years. There is a charge to enter and exploration is on foot without a guide. Some 123 steps lead down the entrance shaft to a platform which gives the first view of the stalactites and stalagmites within the illuminated cavern. Further steps lead down from the platform to a walkway circling the lowest level of the cave. Angled lighting on the best formations brings out the textures and rich colours and helps to illuminate the path around. It is also cool and damp and suitable footwear is advised since the wet rock and the steps can be slippy.

Melissani cave has a collapsed roof and contains a lake. It can only be explored by boat with the help of a guide. The cave is entered by descending down 20 steps to the landing stage where it is necessary to await one of the small boats. Each boat takes around 15 people and is rowed by the boatman using two oars. A trip takes around 10 minutes and the boatman rows across the lake, often through a pool of sunshine, to enter a narrower channel where oars are abandoned for a time in favour of a rope fastened along the cave wall. This section in the darker tunnel is short and then it is a reverse journey back to the landing stage. One or two rock features which form recognisable shapes, like a chicken head, are pointed out along the way. Deep and clear, the waters of the lake are fed from the Katovothres subterranean channel which arises near Argostoli and in turn Melissana waters feed the Karavomylos lake.

Assos

The Theatre, Argostoli

ACCOMMODATION

Hotels

There is a good selection of hotels in the main tourist areas. A directory is available on the internet at **http://www.travel-greece.com/ionian/listzaky.html**

Villas and Apartments

The vast bulk of accommodation on Zakynthos falls into this category. Many, but not all, are in the hands of letting agencies who place them with tour operators. In the early season a lot of apartments stand empty and, even though they may be contracted out, it is still possible to make private arrangements on the spot, sometimes at very attractive rates. A web site listing this type of accommodation can be found at **http://www.zanteweb.gr/lodging.html**

Camping

Camping in areas other than on official camping grounds is not permitted in any part of the island. It is something which the Greek authorities tend to get uptight about, especially in popular tourist regions. For current information on camp sites, contact the **GNTO**.

CAR HIRE

Car hire is popular and many visitors take a car for three or four days which is generally enough to see the various parts of the island. A current driving licence is required for EU nationals and others should have an International Driving Permit. The hirer must be over 21 for a car and 25 for a jeep or a minibus. If there is any intention to take the car on ferries, it must first be sanctioned by the hire company. Some companies do not allow their cars to be taken off the island.

Cars can be hired on the island but a better deal can often be arranged by booking and paying in advance of departure, not necessarily through a tour company but through companies like **Transhire** (☎ 0870 789 8000 & Fax 01923 834 919) who offer good rates and include full insurance and unlimited mileage. These companies operate through an agent on the island and offer rates significantly lower than those available from the agent on the spot.

There is no shortage of car hire companies on the island but advertised car hire rates are very often the basic rates exclusive of insurance, mileage and tax. Third party insurance is compulsory under Greek law and this cost will be added to the hire charge. An additional optional insurance is collision damage waiver (CDW) and it is imperative to take it. This cannot be stressed too strongly. Should you be unfortunate enough to be involved in an accident without CDW insurance and the costs cannot be recovered from a third party then the consequences can be frightening. At best you may be faced with a huge repair bill, at worst you could end up in jail until it is fully paid. On short one or two day hires mileage is limited to 60 miles (100km) per day and a rate applies for excess mileage (kilometres). On top of all this is VAT at 18 per cent.

Tyres and damage to the underside of the car are mostly excluded from insurance cover. Take time when you are accepting the car to inspect the tyres and, if not fully satisfied, don't accept the vehicle. It is worth a moment too to check that lights and indicators are fully operational. Greek law demands that a car must also carry a fire extinguisher, first aid kit and a warning triangle.

Motorcycles

Above comments on insurance apply also to hiring a motorcycle or moped. Insist on a crash helmet since the law says very clearly that these must be worn. Most agencies have helmets now but only produce them if they think that they are about to lose business. Make sure before you depart that the lights and indicators work.

See also Driving on Zakynthos (p77).

CHANGING MONEY

Banks are in extremely short supply outside Zakynthos town but there are plenty of ATMs and exchange bureaux around to compensate. Check that the ATM displays a full range of symbols including Cirrus and Maestro then use your normal bank card and pin number as you would at home. It is the easiest and cheapest way of obtaining cash. Exchange bureaux take traveller's cheques but charge a commission, usually 2per cent, on top of the commission charged by the bank. Normally, the bureaux are open for much longer hours than banks, sometimes extending well into the evening. Hotels also offer exchange facilities but their rates are generally less favourable.

For those travelling into Zakynthos town to use the banks then the opening hours are as follows: Mon-Thurs 8am-2pm, Friday 8am-1.30pm. Post offices sometimes offer exchange facilities and they are open on weekdays from 7.30am-2pm, closed on Saturday and Sunday.

CONSULATES

There are no consuls on the island but the Tourist Police are empowered to issue a temporary exit in the event of a lost or stolen passport. If there is sufficient time, they will fax the Embassy in Athens to obtain a temporary passport.

Nearest foreign Embassies and Consulates are:

Australia
37 D Soutsou Street &
An Tsocha, 15 21 Athens
☎ 01 6447303

Canada
4 I. Genadou Street,
115 21 Athens
☎ 01 7239511-9

Soaking up the sun, Laganas

Banana Beach

New Zealand
15 -17 Toscha Street,
115 12 Athens
☎ 01 6410311-5

UK
Consul
Votsi 2, Patras
☎ 061 276403

USA
Embassy-Consulate
91 Vass. Sophias Avenue,
115 21 Athens
☎ 01 721951-9

CRIME AND THEFT

On an island like Zakynthos, crime and theft levels are low and incidences of violence rare. There is no need to feel threatened in any way, even throughout the evening, but it is sensible to be cautious late at night, especially women on their own.

Many hotels have safety deposit boxes available for guests at a small charge. Otherwise, keep valuables out of sight. This is particularly true if you have a car. Cameras, personal stereos and the like are best carried with you but if you need to leave them in the car make sure they are locked in the boot.

If you are unfortunate enough to suffer a loss through theft or carelessness then report it to the Tourist Police. There is a form to complete if an insurance claim is contemplated.

If your loss includes a passport then you will need to contact the Tourist Police (see Consulates).

CURRENCY & CREDIT CARDS

Greece, as a member of the Economic and Monetary Union (EMU) adopted the euro currency on January 1st, 2002. Their currency, in common with the other 11 participating countries, has notes of value 5, 10, 20, 50, 100, 200 & 500 euros. These are of a standard design throughout the EMU zone. Each euro is divided into 100 cents with coins of 1, 5, 10, 20 and 50 cents. There are also 1 and 2 euro coins. The coins have a standard design on one side and national design on the other. Both the notes and coins are legal tender throughout the EMU zone but the coins of one country might be viewed with suspicion in another.

Travellers cheques, in sterling or euros, and hard currencies are freely accepted at banks, Post Offices and Exchange Bureaux. Credit cards and charge cards are also widely accepted in hotels, shops and restaurants in the main resorts. Visa cards and most bank cards can be used in ATMs.

Always take your passport when changing money. Even though the production of a passport may not be a necessary requirement, the Greeks rely on them as a means of identification. You can expect to be asked for it when purchasing an internal flight ticket. The cost of changing money in terms of commission does vary and it pays to check; normally the cheapest place is at a bank and the worst place is the hotel reception.

DRIVING ON ZAKYNTHOS

Driving on Zakynthos is on the right hand side of the road and overtaking on the left. In the event of an accident where the driver was proven to be on the wrong side of the road, the insurance is invalidated. Unless there are signs indicating otherwise, the speed limits are as follows: built-up areas 31mph (50kph), outside built-up areas 50mph (80kph). Seat belts must be worn by law. The use of main beam headlights in towns and cities is forbidden as is the carrying of petrol in cans.

Unleaded petrol (*amolivthi venzini*) is freely available on Zakynthos. The grades of petrol (*venzini*) normally on offer are unleaded, Super-unleaded and Super at 96/98 octane. Diesel is also widely available and, like petrol, is sold by the litre.

Parking in Zakynthos town is not too much of a problem, either along the front or near the Mole at the north end of the town but can be difficult in the central areas at busy times. It pays to observe street parking restrictions, often ignored by the Greeks, but illegal parking can result in a ticket and a hefty fine. The ticket indicates the amount of the fine and where and when to pay it. The police are not empowered to collect on the spot fines.

With one of the worst accident rates in Europe, driving in Greece demands a cautious attitude from the onset. The discipline shown by the majority of drivers in western European countries, which brings order to traffic flow, is often missing from Greek drivers. Drive with your own safety in mind. Another major hazard is the state of the roads. Potholes are always a danger and can be encountered unexpectedly even on well surfaced roads. A line of rocks on the road guiding you towards the centre is the usual warning of edge subsidence and there will often be no other warning signs. Minor roads, which are well surfaced, may suddenly become unmetalled. Road works may have no hazard warning signs or irregular ones such as a pile of earth or a milk crate with a small flag.

Here is a quick check on some of the hazards frequently encountered: uncertain rights of way, limited road markings, narrow roads, sharp edges, potholes, ill-placed road signs, Greek drivers driving the wrong way through a one-way system, sheep, goats and donkeys, motorcyclists without lights, and pedestrians where there are no footpaths.

Information on all aspects of motoring can be obtained from the:

Automobile Association & Touring Club of Greece,
ELPA, Athens Tower,
2-4, Messogion Street,
15 27 Athens.
☎ 01 7791 615 & 7797 402

Accidents and Legal Advice

In the event of an accident involving personal injury or damage to property, both the law and your insurance require that it is reported to the police (☎ 0671 22200).

ELPA offer free legal advice concerning Greek legislation on car accidents and insurance.

Breakdowns

It is a legal requirement to place a warning triangle 100yds/m behind the car. Next step is to contact the car hire agency or if the car is private, contact Elpa by dialling 104. Elpa has reciprocal arrangements with European motoring organisations, like the British AA.

DISABLED FACILITIES

Whilst there is an awareness of this problem, few practical steps have been taken to improve matters. As yet only international hotels provide anything like adequate facilities. Outside Zakynthos town, very few places have pavements and where present they are often full of trees making passage difficult in places. Ramps up and down pavements are few and far between

ELECTRICITY

Mains electricity is supplied at 220 volts AC. Electrical equipment should be fitted with a continental two pin plug or an appropriate adapter used. A wide selection of adapters for local plugs to inter-change between two and three pin (not UK three pin) are available cheaply on the island.

EMERGENCY TELEPHONE NUMBERS

First point of contact is the police who should be able to offer further guidance. There is no central number, just regional ones:

Police: Laganas 51251
                   Zakynthos Tourist Police 42550
                   Alikes 83217
                   Volimes 31204

Hospital: 42514

ESSENTIAL THINGS TO PACK

Since Greece is a full member of the EU, it is very likely that, should you forget your favourite brand of toothpaste, you will be able to buy it in the shops there. All leading brands of food and products are freely available, give or take some national peculiarities. If you have a favourite brand of tea or tea bags, the easy solution is to

find room for some in your luggage.

There are a few other items which are worth considering if only to save time shopping when you are there:

An electric mosquito repeller and tablets - these are readily available in Greece but small 'travel' types are freely available in U.K. shops which are a convenient size for packing and will last for years. Make sure you buy one with a continental 2 pin plug.

Insect repellent - if you prefer a particular brand, buy it at home. Anthisan cream for insect bites.

Folding umbrella, particularly if you are visiting Zakynthos outside the main season. Rain showers tend to be short and, with the rain falling straight down, an umbrella gives good protection, better than a waterproof which can quickly make you hot and sweaty.

A small rucksack is useful too for general use when heading for the beach or off on a shopping trip.

Only in early or late season is it necessary to take a heavy jumper but it is always useful to take some thinner layers of clothing which you can wear together if necessary. Sometimes it is cool in the evening or you may feel cool after the heat of the sun. If you intend to do any serious walking make sure you have suitable footwear.

Most basic medical requirements, plasters, bandages, headache pills can be bought in chemist shops on Zakynthos. More than that, many drugs normally available in Britain only on prescription can be bought over the counter on demand and at reasonable prices.

Note that codeine and drugs containing codeine are strictly banned in Greece so be sure to exclude these from your luggage.

GREEK TIME

Greek normal time is 2 hours ahead of GMT. The clocks advance one hour for summertime starting the last Sunday in March and ending the last Sunday in October in line with other EU member states.

America and Canada: Greek normal time is ahead of time in America, 7 hours ahead of Eastern Standard, 8 hours ahead of Central, 9 hours ahead of mountain and 10 hours ahead of Pacific Time.

Australia and New Zealand: Greek normal time is 7 hours behind South Australia, 8 hours behind New South Wales, Tasmania and Victoria and 10 hours behind time in New Zealand. These differences relate to GMT.

HEALTH CARE

For minor ailments like headaches, mosquito bites or tummy upsets, head for the chemist shop (*farmakion*). If you need a further supply of prescription drugs make sure to take a copy of your prescription and the chances are that you will be able to get them, and cheaply too. Pharmacies are open normal shop hours and most seem to speak English. Certain chemist shops are on a rota to

Fact File

provide a 24 hour service and information for the nearest is posted in the pharmacy window.

If it is a doctor or dentist you require, the chemist shop should again be able to assist. The island is not short of English speaking doctors and dentists.

Problems really start if hospital treatment is required. European countries have reciprocal arrangements with the Greeks for free medical treatment, subject to certain restrictions. For this reason British visitors should take an E111 form obtained from the Post Office. The story does not end there. To operate the scheme you need to find the local Greek Social Insurance office (IKA) who, after inspecting your E111, will direct you to a registered doctor or dentist. If you are in a region remote from the IKA office in Zakynthos town then you must pay privately for your treatment and present your bills to an IKA official before you leave the island. Up to half your costs may be refunded. The best answer is to ensure that you have adequate holiday insurance cover, although the insurer may still expect to offset some cost by use of the E111 form.

Emergency treatment, sunburn, broken bones etc., is free in state hospitals. The situation is less happy if you require treatment as an in-patient. In many of these hospitals, nursing care is restricted to medical treatment only and it is left to the family to supply general nursing care, drinks, food and even blankets.

It is generally preferable to activate private medical insurance.

HEALTH HAZARDS

Stomach upsets are perhaps the most common ailment. The excessive olive oil used in cooking and over salads can be a cause of queezy stomachs so take care with oily foods, at least to start with. The digestive system adjusts to this within a few days and you can soon eat giant beans swimming in oil without fear. Squeeze plenty of fresh lemon over your food to counter the oil and, if still troubled, an acidic drink, like Coca-Cola, helps to settle things. Drinking wine to excess can cause similar symptoms too. More serious are the upsets caused by bad water and bad food. Generally on Zakynthos it is better to drink bottled water which is freely available and cheap in the shops and supermarkets. Avoiding food poisoning is not always possible but there are elementary precautions that can help. Many tavernas prepare cooked dishes for the lunch time trade and these are left keeping warm until finally sold. If they are still there in the evening, and they often are, avoid them. Ask for something which will require grilling or roasting.

Care is needed on the beach to avoid stings from jelly fish and, in rocky regions, from sea urchins. If you are unlucky enough to have a brush with the latter then it is important to ensure that all the spines are properly removed. Wearing beach shoes will give your feet some protection from stings of this nature.

See also Mosquitoes (p81).

HOLIDAY INSURANCE

Whichever holiday insurance you choose, make sure that the cover for medical expenses is more than adequate. It helps too if there is an emergency 24 hour contact to take care of arrangements, including repatriation if necessary. Injuries caused whilst taking part in certain hazardous pursuits are normally excluded from medical cover. Look carefully at the specified hazardous pursuits; in recent times, injuries caused by riding a moped or motorbike have been added to the list by some insurers.

INTERNATIONAL DIALLING CODES

Codes from Greece are as follows:

UK & Northern Ireland	0044
United States & Canada	001
Australia	0061
New Zealand	0064

See also Telephone Services.

LOST PROPERTY

This should be reported immediately to the Tourist Police in Zakynthos town along the harbour front (☎ 42550). It is particularly important if an insurance claim is to be made.

MAPS

The publisher Road Editions is producing excellent maps for many parts of Greece based on the Hellenic Army maps. These are the most accurate maps available to the general public and there is one for Zakynthos (No 305, 1:60,000) which can be bought on the island or in advance, at a higher price, from **Stamfords** in London or the **Map Shop** in Upton upon Severn.

Generally, road signposting is fairly good on the island with Greek signs displayed first and the Latinised version a little nearer the junction.

MOSQUITOES

Mosquitoes feed most actively at dusk and dawn but they can still be a nuisance throughout the evening and the night. If you sit or dine outside in the evening, particularly near trees, either cover up your arms and legs or use insect repellent. For the hotel room, an electric machine which slowly vaporises a pellet is very effective, especially with the windows closed, and there are sprays available for more instant results if intruders are spotted. Anthisan antihistamine cream is an effective calming treatment for bites, particularly if applied immediately.

Mikro Nisi

MUSEUMS

There is a charge for admission except for some which offer free entrance on a Sunday. Monday is now the general closing day.

Museums are closed too, or open only for a short while, on certain public holidays which include 1 Jan, 25 March, Good Friday and Easter Monday, 1 May and 25 &26 December. In addition they have half-days on Shrove Monday, Whitsunday, August 15th, October 28th and Epiphany, January 6th.

NATIONAL TOURIST OFFICE

In spite of protracted discussions and promises, the Greek National Tourist Office still has no presence on the island.

Leaflets on Zakynthos, the Ionian Islands and general information on Greece is available before departure from the **Greek National Tourist Office**, addresses as follows:

UK and Ireland
4 Conduit Street,
London W1R 0DJ
☎ 0171 734 599

USA
645 Fifth Avenue,
Olympic Tower (5th Floor),
New York NY10022
☎ 421 57777

168 North Michigan Avenue,
Chicago, Illinois 60601
☎ 728 1084

611 West 6th Street,
Suite 2198 Los Angeles,
California 90017 ☎ 626 696

Australia & New Zealand
51-57 Pitt Street, Sydney,
NSW 2000 ☎ 241 1663

NEWSPAPERS & MAGAZINES

The Financial Times, most British newspapers, a selection from European countries and the Herald Tribune are usually available in virtually all centres of tourism. Mostly they are one day late. Expect a fair mark-up in price. The place to look for newspapers is in tourist shops, supermarkets and at kiosks (*periptera*) where you will see them displayed on racks or along the counter.

A selection of English and European magazines is also available.

NIGHTLIFE

Zakynthos has a reasonable amount of nightlife in its major resorts, notably Laganas, Argassi and Tsilivi. This ranges from cocktail bars to music bars, discos, night clubs and the increasingly popular kareoke bars. Music is allowed outside only until midnight but may continue indoors until 2.30am weekdays and 3.30am at weekends. Many tavernas also offer Greek dancing and the inevitable

organised Greek nights with live music, dancing, Greek food and
free wine are available in all resorts.

NUDISM

Topless bathing is commonplace on all public beaches on Zakynthos. Nude bathing is not acceptable on public beaches but is
practised with discretion on some of the more remote and secluded beaches.

PASSPORTS AND JABS

There are no visa requirements for EU citizens or other English
speaking nationals (USA, Australia, Canada, New Zealand) for visits
of up to 3 months. All that is required is a valid passport.
   Certain inoculations are advisable for all travellers (hepatitis A,
tetanus, typhoid and TB) but none is mandatory for Greece.

PETS

Cats and dogs require health and rabies inoculation certificates
issued by a veterinary authority in the country of origin not more
than 12 months (cats 6 months) and not less than 6 days prior to
arrival.

PHARMACIES

Pharmacies open Monday & Wednesday 8am-2.30pm, Tuesday,
Thursday & Friday 8am-2pm & 5-8pm and Saturday 8am-1pm.
There is also a duty rosta for pharmacies so that at least one in the
vicinity is open on Saturday and Sunday. Usually a note on the
door of the pharmacy details the duty chemist.

PHOTOGRAPHY

Signs which show a picture of a camera crossed out indicate a
prohibited area for photography. Notices of this kind are posted
near every military establishment, no matter how small or insigni-
ficant. Disregard this at your peril. The Greeks are still paranoiac
about security and anyone found using a camera in a prohibited
zone faces unpleasant consequences. The photographer is normally
held in custody whilst the film is developed and inspected. It could
mean overnight detention.
   Photography with a camera mounted on a tripod is prohibited in
museums as is the use of flash in some. Video cameras are usually
subject to a fee.
   Outdoors, the light for photography is brilliant. Summer haze can
cause difficulties with distant shots but the use of a UV or Skylight
filter is helpful here. Some of the clearest days occur in spring when
a dry east wind blows. Midday light is harsh and contrasty,

mornings and evening provide the best lighting conditions for serious photography.

POSTAL SERVICES

Post Offices open on weekdays from 7.30am-2pm. They are closed on Saturday and Sunday.

Stamps (*grammatosima*) can be purchased at the post office, sometimes at a special counter, or at a kiosk (*periptero*). They are also available in many shops and some of the larger hotels but at a slightly increased price.

Letters from Greece to overseas destinations are delivered fairly speedily, 4-6 days for Europe, 6-8 for America and longer for Australia and New Zealand. For a speedier delivery, ask for express post on which there is a fairly modest surcharge but it cuts 2-3 days off the delivery time.

A telegram, telex or fax can be sent from the telephone office, the OTE although some tour agency offices also provide a service

PUBLIC HOLIDAYS AND FESTIVALS

The Greek calendar overflows with red letter days; public holidays, saints days and festivals. On public holidays, banks, shops and offices are closed although restaurants and tavernas normally stay open. Public transport is often interrupted too, reverting either to a Sunday service or to none at all. Petrol stations also close for many of the holidays. The days to watch out for are:

- **1 January** - New Year's Day
- **6 January** - Epiphany
- **25 March** - Greek Independence Day
- **Monday before Lent** - Clean Monday
- **April - Good Friday & Easter Monday**
- **1 May** - May Day
- **21 May** - Ionian Day, commemorating union with Greece
  Whit Monday
- **15 August** - Assumption of the Blessed Virgin Mary
- **28 October** - 'Ochi' Day
- **25 December** - Christmas Day
- **26 December** - Boxing Day

Easter is variable and does not always coincide with Easter through-out the rest of Europe.

Name-days are one reason why the calendar is so full of cele-brations. It has been a long tradition for Greeks to ignore birthdays and to celebrate instead the special day of their saint, and there are a lot of saints. If you see people wandering around with cake boxes neatly tied with fancy ribbon, or bunches of flowers or unusual activity around one of the many churches, then the chances are that it is a name-day. The custom is for the person celebrating to offer hospitality to friends, to neighbours and to almost anyone who will

partake of a little ouzo and refreshments.
Some of the big name days to watch out for are:

- **23 April** - St George's day; all Georges everywhere celebrate their special day but in addition it is also the national day of Greece.
- **21 May** - Saints Konstantinos and Eleni.
- **29 June** - St Peter and St Paul.
- **15 August** - Assumption of the Blessed Virgin Mary. This is the day when millions of Marias celebrate and is an important day in the religious calendar often marked by local pilgrimages or festivals.
- **8 November** - for all Michaels and Gabriels.
- **6 December** - the feast of St Nicholas.

Easter, the biggest and the most important celebration of the year and the arrival of Carnival time starts the long build up. This festival takes place throughout the three weeks before Lent and may commence as early as late January. Fancy dress is an important part of the tradition throughout the whole of Greece. It arises from the period of Turkish occupation when the Greeks were banned from conducting these celebrations. Driven under cover, festivities continued with people disguised to prevent recognition. Now it is firmly rooted into the custom and fancy dress and costumes are worn at all events. The children wander the streets in fancy dress and traditionally show defiance by wearing their disguises on the last school day of Carnival.

All this comes to an abrupt end with a complete change of mood on 'Clean Monday' (*Kathari Deutera*), the Monday before Lent. This is a public holiday when families traditionally exodus to the country to fly kites and to picnic, which mostly means heading to a taverna. Special meat-free menus are the order of the day.

It is back to the quiet life throughout Lent which is still strictly observed by many, especially in country regions. Serious preparations for Easter start on Maundy Thursday. How hens are persuaded to lay so actively for the occasion remains a mystery but shoppers are out buying eggs, not by the tens but by the hundreds. The rest of the day is spent in boiling the eggs and dying them red in the process. The colour red is supposed to have protective powers and the first egg dyed belongs to the Virgin.

Good Friday is a day of complete fast and widely observed. In tourist regions tavernas are open and life goes on as normal but in country areas it can be difficult or impossible to find food. Yellow or brown 'impure' candles are on sale everywhere ready for the evening church service. The sombre mood of the day is heightened by the continual tolling of church bells. It is a day for remembering the dead; graves are visited and wreaths are laid. In the evening, the burial of Christ is the most moving and widely attended service in the whole of the Greek Orthodox calendar. The *Epitaphios*, the funeral bier of Christ, is centre stage in the services which start around 9 o'clock in the evening. Garlanded with fresh flowers and with a gilded canopy, the Epitaphios bearing the coffin of Christ is ceremoniously taken from church in dignified candlelit procession followed by silent mourners and accompanied by bands playing solemn music. The processions from all the local churches meet in the town square for a further short service. This is the most poignant moment of the evening, cafés close, tavernas close and there is not one Greek who would willingly miss it. The processions return slowly to their churches, stopping at each street corner for a short prayer.

Zakynthos has a unique custom relating to Good Friday which is found nowhere else in Greece. From the night of Good Friday until dawn on Saturday, practical jokes are the order of the night and the following day it is not unusual to see shops with their signs switched over to something quite inappropriate.

Saturday brings an air of expectancy. For the evening service, yellow candles are replaced with white. Funereal drapes are re-moved in the churches and decorations of laurel and myrtle take their place. In dimly lit churches everywhere, services begin. Slowly the light intensity increases reaching full brightness at midnight when priests triumphantly chant 'Christ is risen' (*Christos anesti*). The sanctuary doors open to show that the Epitaphios is empty. Light from the priest's candle is passed to the congregation and that flame is rapidly passed from candle to candle until it reaches the waiting crowds outside. Fire crackers drown the clamour of the church bells as the crowd erupts in joyous celebration and greetings of 'Christos anesti' ring out loudest of all. The crowds disperse shortly carefully protecting their burning candle; it is a good omen to enter the home with the flame still burning and make a sooty sign of the cross on the door lintel.

Sunday is a day.of.out-and-out rejoicing. The big occasion of the day is roasting the lamb or goat. Charcoal fires are lit early in the morning and the spit roasting is done with loving care over some 5 hours with copious quantities of ouzo or retsina to help things along. All those red eggs now appear and are used in friendly competition. Each contestant taps their egg hard enough to break an opponent's but not their own.

Easter Monday has no special ceremonies or rituals and passes as any normal public holiday.

Cultural events

Religious fairs, *panayiria*, are commonplace in the summer months. Panayiria are a celebration of the name day of a particular church or monastery and usually held in the vicinity of the establishment. Celebrations are colourful, often beginning on the eve of the name-day and continue throughout the actual day. Eating, drinking and dancing are central to any celebration for the Greeks so the barbe-cue is certain to be in operation. When the crowds are big enough, the vendors join in selling just about anything, baubles, bangles and beads.

Ag Dionysos, the island's patron saint, is celebrated twice a year, on 24 August and again on 17 December. The island's other major saint's day is held on 15 August at Macherado to celebrate Ag Mavra.

A word of warning too. Each town and village has its own saint's day and sometimes, depending on the local whim and the phase of the moon, a holiday is called. This decision is often not taken until the day before so there is no way you can plan for such eventualities.

PUBLIC TOILETS

The most usual sign is WC with figures to indicate ladies (*gynaikon*) and gents (*andron*). Cafés provide the best hope of toilets even though it may be necessary to purchase a drink.

PUBLIC TRANSPORT

Buses

The bus service on Zakynthos is good and it offers a reliable way to see the island. The biggest problem is that buses on popular routes get overcrowded in season and it may be difficult to board one at an intermediate stop.

Printed timetables are usually available from the bus station. The frequency of services is much less in winter but builds up as the tourist season gets underway. Throughout May the timetable changes weekly until the service reaches its maximum frequency sometime in June which is then held until early September. The timetable holds equally from Monday through to Saturday but Sunday sees a reduction in the number of buses to about half.

Taxis

Taxis are freely available in Zakynthos town and most tourist resorts.

Greek taxi drivers are not the most honest in the world and it pays either to check the price before the journey, if it is for a lengthy ride, or better still, insist that the meter be used. This displays the cumulative fare in drachmas. The rates of charges and surcharges are all fixed. Legitimate small surcharges are allowed for a sizeable piece of luggage, for attending an airport or port for the benefit of passengers, and for late night or very early morning travel. Surcharges are permitted too at holiday times, especially Christmas and Easter. Picking up a second fare is allowed too so you may find yourself sharing a taxi.

SHOPPING

Regulations on opening hours have changed recently to adjust to market needs. Different regions have their own views on this so there is now greater confusion than ever over opening times. Big supermarkets and department stores open: Monday-Friday 8am-

8.pm, Saturday 8am-3pm. Other shops open Monday & Wednesday 8am-2.30pm, Tuesday, Thursday, & Friday 8am-2pm & 5-8pm and Saturday 8am-1pm.

In tourist areas, shopping hours are much more relaxed. Tourist shops and supermarkets in particular are open all day long but butchers, bakers and the like tend to observe more restricted hours.

SPORTS & PASTIMES

Go-karting

Zakynthos Karting Club, near Vanato, open 9.30am-3pm & 5-11pm.

Horse riding

There are opportunities for horse riding and schools are located near most major resorts.

Sailing

There are no major marinas on the island but speed boats are available for hire at most resorts.

Scuba diving

Strictly prohibited unless in the control of a recognised diving school and only in designated areas. With so many antiquities in the waters around Greece, it is forbidden to remove anything from the sea bed and infringements normally result in a prison sentence.

Swimming

There is good swimming off many beaches on the island but there is not always a system of warning flags to indicate unsafe conditions. It is absolutely essential to use common sense when the sea is rough or strong currents are flowing and avoid taking unnecessary risks.

Tennis

Courts are mostly to be found in better class hotels but some allow non residents to use the facilities for a charge.

Water-skiing & Jet-skiing

Available at some of the larger resorts as well as parascending.

Windsurfing

Many of the small bays and coves are ideally suited to this sport and boards can be hired in most holiday resorts. Lessons for beginners are generally available too at rates which are still very reasonable.

SUNBATHING

Sunburn and sunstroke can easily spoil your holiday and considerable care needs to be exercised, especially in the early days. The sun is very burning even on a hazy day so great care is needed in protecting yourself and high factor sun creams should be used. Crawling beneath a parasol isn't necessarily the full answer since the sun's rays reflect to some extent from the sand. Avoid, if possible, sunbathing in the middle of the day, from 10am until around 2.00pm when the sun it at its highest and most direct. Sun creams help considerably but, at least for the first few days, take some very light clothing to cover up and control the exposure of your skin to the sun. A slowly acquired tan lasts longer.

Even mild sunburn can be painful and may cause a chill feeling but if fever, vomiting or blistering occur then professional help is essential.

TELEPHONE SERVICES

Hotels usually offer a telephone service, often from the room, but expect to pay a premium for the convenience.

Telephone booths on the island have now been modernised to take card phones and these are both convenient and economical. Cards, loaded with 100 units, are available often from the shop or *periptero* nearest the booth and the cost per unit is exactly the same as the OTE (Telecommunications Office) charge. There is an OTE office in Zakynthos town where metered phones are available with a pay at the desk system.

In the main holiday resorts a number of tourist agencies offer a telephone service and often call themselves telephone exchanges. Although sometimes convenient, they are run for profit so expect to pay a higher rate.

See also International Dialling Codes (p81).

TIPPING

There are no hard and fast rules on tipping, especially since bills by law already include a 17 per cent service. Normally, the Greeks simply leave behind the small change after a meal and perhaps the best guide is to reward only for good service in a restaurant. Taxi drivers expect a tip as does the chamber maid in the hotel otherwise it is entirely by discretion.

WATER

Sources of drinking water vary on the island and all should be regarded as not suitable to drink unless otherwise advised. Bottled water is freely available.

INDEX

LANDMARK
VISITORS GUIDES

US & British
Virgin Islands

Antigua
& Barbuda

Bermuda

Barbados

St Lucia

US & British VI*
ISBN: 1 901522 03 2
256pp,
UK £11.95 US $15.95

Antigua & Barbuda*
ISBN: 1 901522 02 4
96pp,
UK £5.95 US $12.95

Bermuda*
ISBN: 1 901522 07 5
160pp,
UK £7.95 US $12.95

Barbados*
ISBN: 1 901522 32 6
144pp,
UK £6.95 US $12.95

St Lucia*
ISBN: 1 901522 82 2
144pp,
UK £6.95 US $13.95

**Pack
2 months
into
2 weeks
with your
Landmark
Visitors
Guides**

Jamaica

Orlando
& Central Florida

Florida:
Gulf Coast

Florida:
The Keys

Jamaica*
ISBN: 1 901522 31 8
144pp
UK £6.95 US $12.95

Orlando*
ISBN: 1 901522 22 9
256pp,
UK £9.95 US $15.95

Florida: Gulf Coast*
ISBN: 1 901522 01 6
160pp
UK £7.95 US $12.95

Florida: The Keys*
ISBN: 1 901522 21 0
160pp,
UK £7.95 US $12.95

Dominican
Republic

Gran
Canaria

Algarve

Kefalonia

Northern
Cyprus

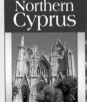

Dominican Republic*
ISBN: 1 901522 08 3
160pp,
UK £7.95 US $12.95

Gran Canaria*
ISBN: 1 901522 19 9
160pp
UK £7.95 US $12.95

Algarve
ISBN: 1 901522 92 X
112pp,
UK £6.50

Kefalonia
ISBN: 1 901522 96 2
96pp,
UK £6.50

North Cyprus
ISBN: 1 901522 51 2
192pp
UK £8.95

Provence*
ISBN: 1 901522 45 8
240pp,
UK £10.95 US $17.95

Côte d'Azur*
ISBN: 1 901522 29 6
144pp,
UK £6.95 US $13.95

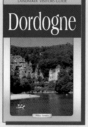

Dordogne
ISBN: 1 901522 67 9
176pp,
UK £9.95

Vendée
ISBN: 1 901522 76 X
160pp,
UK £7.95

Languedoc
ISBN: 1 901522 79 2
144pp,
UK £6.95

Bruges*
ISBN: 1 901522 66 0
96pp,
UK £5.95 US $10.95

Ticino
ISBN: 1 901522 74 1
192pp
UK £8.95

Italian Lakes*
ISBN: 1 901522 11 3
240pp,
UK £10.95 US $15.95

Riga*
ISBN: 1 901522 59 8
160pp,
UK £7.95

Cracow
ISBN: 1 901522 54 7
160pp,
UK £7.95

Iceland*
ISBN: 1 901522 68 7
192pp,
UK £12.95 US $17.95

New Zealand*
ISBN: 1 901522 36 9
320pp
UK £12.95 US $18.95

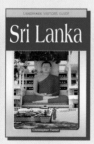

Sri Lanka
ISBN: 1 901522 37 7
192pp,
UK £9.95

India: Kerala
ISBN: 1 901522 16 4
256pp,
UK £10.99

India: Goa
ISBN: 1 901522 23 7
160pp,
UK £7.95

Prices subject to alteration from time to time

Published in the UK by
Landmark Publishing Ltd,
Ashbourne Hall, Cokayne Ave, Ashbourne, Derbyshire DE6 1EJ England
Tel: (01335) 347349 Fax: (01335) 347303
e-mail: sales@landmarkpublishing.co.uk
website: www.landmarkpublishing.co.uk

ISBN: 1 901522 97 0

Print: Gutenberg Press Ltd, Malta
Design: James Allsopp
Cartography: Mark Titterton
Editor: Kay Coulson

Front cover: Mikronisi
Back cover, top: Zakynthos Town
Back cover, bottom: Pilarinos, nr Mikro Nisi

Picture Credits:
All photographs are supplied by the authors.

DISCLAIMER
While every care has been taken to ensure that the information in this book
is as accurate as possible at the time of publication, the publishers
and authors accept no responsibility for any loss, injury or
inconvenience sustained by anyone using this book.